# The Dynamic of Service

# The
# Dynamic
## of
# Service

A Handbook on Reaping the Harvest

A. PAGET WILKES

*foreword by*

JIM WILSON

Published by Community Christian Ministries
P.O. Box 9754, Moscow, Idaho 83843
208.883.0997 | www.ccmbooks.org

A. Paget Wilkes, *The Dynamic of Service: A Handbook on Reaping the Harvest*

Copyright © 1921 by Japan Evangelistic Band. Used by permission.

First edition published 1921 by Japan Evangelistic Band.
First Community Christian Ministries edition published 1993.
Second Community Christian Ministries edition published 1999.
Third Community Christian Ministries edition published 2019.

Unless otherwise noted, all Scripture quotations are from the New King James Version®. Copyright ©1982 by Thomas Nelson, Inc. Used by permission. All rights reserved..

Scripture quotations marked KJV are from the King James Version.

Cover design by Forrest Dickison.
Interior design by Valerie Anne Bost.
Printed in the United States of America.

All rights reserved. No part of this publication may be reproduced, stored in a retrieval system, or transmitted in any form by any means, electronic, mechanical, photocopy, recording, or otherwise, without prior permission of the author, except as provided by USA copyright law.

19  20  21  22  23  24  25  26       9  8  7  6  5  4  3  2  1

# Contents

Foreword to the Third CCM Edition.................. vii

Biographical Sketch............................... xiii

Introduction ........................................ 1

1 : The Dynamic of a Commission.................... 3

2 : Diagnosis of Man: The Desires ................. 17

3 : Diagnosis of Man: The Understanding .......... 29

4 : Diagnosis of Man: The Will .................... 43

5 : Ministry and Witness .......................... 55

6 : The Commission ............................... 75

7 : The Sense of Need ............................ 93

8 : The Sense of Sin..............................111

9 : The Minimum of Truth .......................127

10 : The Minimum of Works......................143

11 : Salvation....................................157

12 : Idolatry .....................................169

13 : Conclusion ..................................181

# Foreword

TO THE THIRD CCM EDITION

*The Dynamic of Service* has been a great blessing to me several times. It was given to me by my future wife, Bessie Dodds, in 1951. Bessie was principal of the Women's Bible School in Yokohama, Japan. While in language school, she had lived with two Japan Evangelistic Band missionaries, Irene Webster-Smith and Jean McCormack. Miss Webster-Smith introduced me to Bessie in November 1950.

The second time I read *The Dynamic of Service* was in Yokohama, where we were living in the fall of 1955. The principles taught in this book caught my attention in such a way that I knew they could be put into effect immediately. I prayed for such an opportunity. This opportunity was given to me almost at once on the *USS Hancock,* an American aircraft carrier then in Yokosuka, Japan. One week before Thanksgiving Day 1955, I was given orders to report to Commander Carrier Division Five riding the *Hancock* for six months' temporary duty. We got underway on Friday and arrived at Iwakuni at the western end of the Inland Sea on Saturday. On Sunday, the "possibility of an immediate harvest" came true with the first of about three dozen officers and men passing from death to life during the six weeks I was on the *Hancock.*

Several years later, in the summer of 1959, I gave a copy to a young "Christian" midshipman starting his second year at the U.S. Naval Academy. His summer cruise was to be part of the opening of the St. Lawrence Seaway. I gave him *The Dynamic of Service* hoping it would help him in evangelism as it had helped me.

He became a very effective evangelist. It was not until 1963 that I found out that he himself had been converted reading the book on that summer cruise. He has been in the presence of the Lord since 1964.

*The Dynamic of Service* consists of a series of talks given at a summer resort in Japan. It was originally published in 1920. After reading it three times, Dr. R.A. Torrey said that if he could put only one other book besides the Bible into the hands of his students, it would be *The Dynamic of Service.*

Here is a quotation from B. Godfry Buxton's foreword to Paget Wilkes' biography, *Dynamic:*

> One outstanding feature of his ministry was that he drew from Scripture such clear proof that the death of Christ was wholly sufficient to meet every requirement of both saint and sinner before God, that faith became spontaneous. Another feature was that his converts stood and matured. Why was this? I think it was because he had so tremendous a gift of presenting the living Christ that it was easy to believe that He could meet your need, however impossible it had seemed to you beforehand.

The following quotations are taken from *Ablaze for God: The Life Story of Paget Wilkes* by his sister Mary W. Dunn Pattison.

> Away back in 1895, when I was recovering from flu, I amused and profited myself by reading *From Sunrise Land,* that most interesting, profitable and humbling book on Japanese life. Propped up by pillows in our drawing-room at home, I can see myself so plainly. When I came to pp. 142–3, where Miss Wilson Carmichael tells of three student enquirers—nameless withal, I put down my book, and did what she asked. "Pray for them," she said. I quote

her words: "Will you not stop, even now as you read this and pray an earnest Amen?" That I did and more! I spent five minutes if my memory serves me aright for those three souls. And what of them to-day? One of them is cold, dead, and unsaved still. The second was converted through Miss Evans. The third was Mr. Kano! At my first meeting in Japan, the Lord gave me a soul, that soul was Mr. Kano. How little did I guess that I should be the one to answer my own prayer! My cup runneth over.

Miss Amy Wilson Carmichael, writing later of this incident, said:

Forty-three years ago I gave a New Testament to a Japanese student, and said, "It will be seed." I told of this in a home letter, and that letter was read by an undergraduate at Oxford. He stopped reading, and, as he said afterwards, "put in five minutes of real praying for that student." Two or three years passed and he went to Japan as a missionary. The first man he was used to win for Christ, so I heard later, was the student for whom he had prayed. That undergraduate was Paget Wilkes.

We have changed words of English spelling to American spelling. We also changed the quotations from the

Authorized Version to the New King James Version. However, when Mr. Wilkes was making a point based on the wording of the King James Version, we did not change the quotation.

JIM WILSON
Moscow, Idaho
2018

# Biographical Sketch

In March 1892, F. B. Meyer spoke on the "Work of the Holy Spirit." It was at this meeting that 21–year-old Paget Wilkes received Jesus Christ. His life was changed. Although his father was a pastor in the Church of England, Paget had known that he himself was not a Christian. It was his stepmother and her enthusiastic friends who talked with him and later invited him to Ipswich to hear F.B. Meyer. Paget had said earlier in response to all their talk, "If I ever become a Christian, I will keep quiet about it."[1]

That fall, Paget "went up" to Oxford, where he became involved in the Oxford Inter-Collegiate Christian Union. It was at Lincoln College where Paget became interested in John Wesley's writings.

1  Information for this biographical sketch is taken from the short biography *Dynamic: Paget Wilkes of Japan* by LR. Govan Stewart.

One day, one of his friends asked him, "I say, Paget, do you tackle everyone who comes into your rooms about his soul?"

"Yes,' answered Paget, "if he comes in alone. Not if he is with another fellow."

If he was assailed at the university, like most young men are, by intellectual problems and moral temptations, there is no sign that his faith was ever moved from "the impregnable rock of Holy Scripture." Two principles which he practiced kept him straight. One was his daily, early-morning time with the Lord. The second was his commitment to evangelism.

In April 1897, Paget graduated from Oxford with a second in Classical Greats. He married Gertrude Barthrope in July. Paget was turned down for missionary work in Africa because he was committed to the teachings of John Wesley. He was invited by Barclay Buxton of the Church Missionary Society to work with him in Matsuye, Japan, and they sailed for Japan in August.

Paget had known Gertrude and corresponded with her for most of his five years at Oxford. When he first met her at a Christian meeting in Manchester, he was attracted to her by her graceful movements, ladylike bearing, her love for God, and her alertness to all that was going on. Their correspondence had to do with things concerning the kingdom of God.

Although Paget was an English gentleman, he became very Japanese. He gained a wide vocabulary and great speaking ability, with no accent. The Japanese language has a different vocabulary for women than for men. It is also filled with honorifics, meaning your language varies depending on the status of the person to whom you are speaking. Paget Wilkes could speak and identify with all classes of Japanese.

Paget and Gertrude spent four years working with Barclay Buxton in Matsuye. One evening at a meeting where he was the only European present, Paget said he experienced what he had previously believed—full salvation. The practice and teaching of evangelism took up the rest of his life.

Although God had done a great work in Matsuye, Barclay Buxton went home to England, not to return to Japan except for visits. On the Wilkes' first furlough, they realized the work in Japan would change with new leadership. Liberalism was already present in the Church Missionary Society and in Japan. Paget Wilkes was concerned. Here is his solution to the problem: "I believe the answer to liberal theology and rationalistic criticism with its blight is the outpouring of the Holy Spirit. And may God use us to bring it about!"

He spent time in his study to pray for Japan and to ponder over the promises of the Word. Fifteen months had passed since their return to England for furlough, and still there was no clear light on the future. At that time, Paget wrote,

> The first need of Japan is for the preaching of
> a real salvation able to reach the lowest and

vilest of men. It seems to be taken for granted that we can never expect anyone to be saved in a heathen land prior to a considerable period of instruction in the principles of Christianity. This appears both reasonable and ordinary common sense, and yet one feels instinctively that there must be a way for a helpless drunkard, a derelict on his way to commit suicide, a criminal condemned to death, and such other, to receive enough instruction in the elements of the Gospel to allow for them entering into the experience of salvation immediately and without delay. As one studies the Scriptures, it seems perfectly plain that the stories of the woman of Samaria, the thief on the cross, the Philippian jailer and others, warrant optimism along this line.

In my first few years of service, I have put this to the test and found it possible. I realize that there are not wanting missionaries and Japanese who believe as I do; and if a band of evangelists, foreign and Japanese, could be raised up who would specialize and stress this phase of truth untrammeled by considerations of ecclesiastical organizations, it might be a great blessing to the whole church of Christ in Japan and help to prove in practical fashion that truth of our proposition that when men's hearts have been prepared by sin, suffering, trouble, and despair, there can be an immediate harvest.

The second great need of Japan is that young converts should know the power of the Holy Spirit to uphold them and to enable them to testify to others. This being so, how important it is to forward conventions for the promotion of Scriptural holiness. If the ministry of the ordinary churches is deficient in this respect (and it certainly is), the simplest way would be to conduct conventions here and there to which Christians of all denominations could come and so hear of the fullness of salvation in Christ Jesus. The value and importance of this method was impressed on my mind by what I saw of Mr. Buxton's work at Matsuye itself in the early days of his ministry.

Japan's greatest need, however, is for evangelists from her own people, full of the Holy Ghost. The best and most permanent thing a missionary can do is to train men to be soul winners and men of prayer. Both the Lord Himself and His servant Paul trained workers by having them with them and letting them share in the work itself. This Mr. Buxton did, and the men whom he trained have been an untold blessing to Japan. A Bible School where a thorough knowledge of the Scriptures would be given, combined with practical training in dealing with souls, open-air work, and house-to-house visiting, is the chief requisite for making evangelists; for the primary need of Japan at this stage is not for a highly educated and cultured pastorate, but for red-hot evangelists, filled with the Spirit and with the Word.

The Japan Evangelistic Band was formed with like-minded people at home praying, headed up by Barclay Buxton in England and a group of Japanese Christians in Japan. Kobe became the Band's headquarters, and Paget directed the work for the next twenty-one years. He relinquished the leadership to James Cuthbertson in 1923, after which he had a greater harvest of souls, and a greater blessing to his fellow believers and to the Bible School students.

The last years of Paget's life were spent in international ministry in China, Switzerland, Canada, the United States, South Africa, and England. He died on October 5, 1934, after spending a quiet day with his wife. He was 63.

# Introduction

The responsibility of service is truly a dynamic to the soul. There are few things that move the hearts and minds of men more effectively than the sense of such responsibility. So long as the Christian's ideal is merely to live in peace and "charity with his neighbor," without any realization of his responsibility towards his soul, it is more than likely that he will make but little progress in the way of holiness and will, moreover, be ignorant of his own state before God. His spiritual bankruptcy hardly becomes apparent. As soon, however, as he begins to understand that he is "his brother's keeper," that no man lives unto himself, and that the humblest Christian, as in the early Church, is responsible for bringing men to

Christ, then he is also made aware of his own poverty. The demand for service proves a dynamic indeed; and he bestirs himself to seek and find, and so become fitted for the performance of his duty—the solemn, yet blessed, duty of saving men!

I am well aware that, though my ministry has covered nearly twenty-five years, it has been largely confined to the limits of one country; and hence much that I have said may not be applicable to other lands. I hope, however, that the statement of general principles and my attempt to concentrate and focus the attention on the vital issues of things may prove of some value, even to workers in countries where other conditions obtain. I send forth this little volume in prayer blended with praise and gratitude that God has allowed me in some feeble measure to be the instrument in His hands of gathering souls from the whitened harvest-fields of Japan.

PAGET WILKES  
Kobe, Japan  
1920

CHAPTER 1
# The Dynamic of a Commission

Then I preached Christ, and when she heard the story,
Oh! is such triumph possible to men?
Hardly, my King, had I beheld Thy glory,
Hardly had known Thine excellence till then.
Then with a rush the intolerable craving
Shivers throughout me like a trumpet call,
Oh! to save these; to perish for their saving;
Die for their life; be offered for them all.
  *—from the poem "St. Paul" by F. W. H. Meyer*

To understand the secret of that magnificent life—the life of the Apostle Paul—we naturally turn to its beginnings. There at the very threshold we are admitted to the audience chamber of his Divine Master, and with him listen to the greatest commission ever given to perhaps the greatest human soul. And yet this commission is for every true servant of Christ, who like the Apostle has cried, "Who art Thou, Lord?" and "What wilt Thou have me to do?"

That commission changes not. It is the same through all time. Thousands all down the centuries have heard it, responded to it, and have gone forth to tell and suffer and die, as did the great Apostle, who first received it from the lips of the Risen and Ascended Redeemer.

In the terms of the commission is set forth the work which every missionary of the Cross has to accomplish. "But rise and stand on your feet; for I have appeared to you for this purpose, to make you a minister and a witness both of the things which you have seen and of the things which I will reveal to you . . . I send you [to the Gentiles], to open their eyes and to turn them from darkness to light, and from the power of Satan to God, that they may receive forgiveness of sins and an inheritance among those who are sanctified by faith in Me" (Acts 26:16, 18).

## The Honor of the Ministry

I have appeared to you . . . to make you a minister . . . (Acts 26:16)

When the angel visited Cornelius, he was able to tell him that his alms and prayers were accepted of God, but added in effect: "I cannot tell you the way of salvation; I cannot communicate to you the gift of eternal life. If you want to know that, you must send to a saved sinner, named Simon Peter."

The angels have no experience of pardoning and regenerating grace. They have never felt rebellion in their hearts; they have never known the mystery of reconciliation; never been plucked from the burning; never been lifted from the slough of sin; never felt the Spirit within, crying, "Abba, Father." How, then, shall they speak of these things to men? How shall they be able to communicate eternal life to dead souls? But to us it is given to be ministers of the grace of God. A friend of mine once observed, "If God gave the command to angels to evangelize the world, heaven would be empty in five minutes."

## The Condition of the Ministry

For I have appeared to you for this purpose, to make you a minister and a witness . . . of the things which you have seen. (Acts 26:16)

In order to be a minister, one needs first of all to be a witness—one who has seen, heard, and known.

That great man of God, John Smith, in the early part of the 19th century once said,

> No man feels the value of the soul of another who has not been made sensible of the worth of his own soul. No man discerns the malignity of sin in the world who has not yet felt its bitterness and terror in his own heart. No man is awake to the peril of the ungodly who has not

trembled under the sense of personal danger. No man forms a correct estimate of the value of the Atonement who has not had the Blood of Christ sprinkled on his own conscience. Here is a deep secret, and one that is absolutely indispensable for the work of soul winning. To put it briefly, we may say that the one task that we are called upon to accomplish is to convict men of sin and then to convince them of the love of God in Christ.

The Lord Jesus appeared to Paul that He might make him a *witness*. Unless our Divine Lord has in some form appeared to us, humbling us in the dust before Him, our ministry will be no ministry at all, but the telling of what to the hearer will sound as "idle tales," "sounding brass," and "tinkling cymbals."

That it is sadly possible to be ordained to the ministry and yet to be in utter darkness of soul, unable to be a witness, we are constantly seeing to our sorrow. The following testimony from one who is now a humble, devoted minister of the Gospel is a sample, I fear, of many, even in the mission field, who are in like case. I shall let him tell his story in his own words.

> I went from the college to my work in the M- district. Soon after getting there, I began to be exercised in my heart about salvation through the Cross of Jesus, and I discovered that I had no

definite experience myself and hence no power to preach it to others. I was deeply tormented by my conscience and searched my notebooks and commentaries, which I had been studying all the five years; but alas! I searched in vain. The more I searched, the more obscure the whole matter became; I could find no peace. After spending one year in this miserable condition, I married; and at the wedding service I recalled the sins of my youth, before I had ever heard of Christ, but I knew nothing of their forgiveness through the Cross. I spent another six months in this condition, when at last I unburdened my heart to a friend. He told me that I had never really repented and that I had no living faith in the Blood of Jesus. I saw and knew that it was true. There and then I yielded to God, repented of my sins, and by faith obtained the witness that I was pardoned from all my transgressions, and so entered into the joy of salvation.

## The Task: The Awakening of the Soul
... to open their eyes ... (Acts 26:18)

We pass on now to the task itself. When we use the expression *conversion* or "the salvation of the soul," it is well to know exactly what is intended thereby. A true conversion means a complete renovation of the whole man—a new creation wherein all the faculties of man are transfigured and changed. In the commission given to St. Paul, this is exactly what we find to be the task set before him. The desires are to be awakened, the understanding enlightened, the will converted, the conscience purified, and the affections renewed. Here, then, is our first task—the awakening of the desires. And yet before we can undertake it, we must be assured that the desires of the unregenerate man, who, to use the language of Scripture, is "dead in trespasses and sins," are debased and depraved, and, furthermore, that men are ignorant of the fact. Like the man with the muckrake, they know nothing of the crown above them. They desire only carnal pleasure and carnal delight. The sticks and straws and rubble of a perishing world are the only things that to them appear of any worth. Our business is to open their eyes, that they may see that these things are no pearls at all, except to swine, and cause them to desire the true, the imperishable, and the divine.

In some respects, this task is far more difficult in heathen lands than in a so-called Christian country. Of course, the human soul is everywhere fast asleep in the arms of the wicked one, whether in England or China, but the means at our disposal for awakening them in heathendom are fewer. Unless we are deeply impressed in our own minds of the need of man, we shall only play at being soldiers.

It is not too much to say that the cause of almost all heresy and unscriptural teaching on the great themes of the Christian faith is to be found in erroneous views of the state, need, and danger of man. If he is not a rebel, he needs no reconciliation; not a slave, then no redemption; not a sinner, then no forgiveness; not depraved, then no sanctification. A divine Savior and His atonement are impertinent superfluities!

Our first task, then, is to get men awakened, i.e., made conscious of their need and sin, and show them that their desperate zeal to get rich and be great in this world is but a muckrake after all. And yet, at the same time, we have to beware of resting there. One who is now a devoted servant of Christ told me not long since of his deep conviction of sin for two whole years. He was thoroughly awakened, and in his distress called on a pastor of a church in Formosa to show him the way of salvation. The only reply he got to his anxious inquiry was, "Young man, you are like a fish in the sea looking for water." Utterly amazed, he looked up and said, "What do you mean by that—that I am saved already?" Receiving a reply in the affirmative, he turned away in despair, saying, "Well, if I am saved, everybody is." Fortunately, God led him to a wiser counselor, through whom he found the path of life, and was soon rejoicing in God his Savior.

## The Task: The Enlightenment of the Understanding
. . . to turn them from darkness to light . . . (Acts 26:18)

Our next task is to enlighten. Many a man has been thoroughly awakened to his need and danger, but has swiftly sunk to sleep again because he has not been enlightened.

This task is not an easy one in a heathen land. There is not even a theoretical knowledge of God, and hence none of sin in its deepest meaning. The knowledge of vice and crime there may be; but of sin against a holy God, none whatever. The words *forgiveness, pardon, justification,* are idle sounds. They have no content and no meaning.

It is this state of things that seems to make a long period of instruction, prior to the exercise of a living faith, absolutely imperative. And yet when a poor drunkard or would-be suicide or criminal comes to us conscious of his or her need—and, thank God, we have had many such—are we to give them the stone of a six months' study in theology for the bread of a present and immediate salvation? Verily, nay! There must be a way—and, thank God, there is—of so enlightening an awakened soul that he may at once enter in and be saved.

The mark of a great preacher in heathen lands is his ability to know just how much content it is necessary to put into the mind of the inquirer before it can be used as a lever to move the heart. I have been amazed again and again at the truth of those words: "The entrance of Your words gives light" (Psalm 119:130).

One who is now a very earnest evangelist stands out very forcibly in my mind. Never having heard a word of Christianity before, he was one night on his way to a house of ill fame, when, attracted by our singing in the open air, he came and stood outside the gathering. As he approached, he heard these words: "For the message of the cross is foolishness to those who are perishing, but to us who are being saved it is the power of God" (1 Cor. 1:18). In a moment, the thought passed through his mind: "Well, it's foolishness to me; I guess, then, I am perishing." Thoroughly awakened by the Spirit of God, he followed us to the hall, and within one short hour was enlightened enough through the Word, as explained by one of our workers, to believe unto salvation. He never went back from that blessed day when in one short hour he was awakened, enlightened, converted, pardoned, and made a new creature in Christ Jesus.

## The Task: The Conversion of the Will

... to turn them ... from the power of Satan to God ... (Acts 26:18)

The third step in the salvation of the soul is repentance. Repentance, of course, is not salvation, though absolutely indispensable thereto.

1) The first of these two ideas as represented to us is *to turn man from the power of Satan*. Behind the depraved desires, the darkened understanding, the seared conscience, and the enslaved will, there stands Satan, the arch-enemy of the human soul. It is with him we have to deal. No man has ever yet been a winner of souls who has not known and believed in the existence of the devil. This conviction is absolutely essential; it drives us to prayer and makes us cry, "Avenge us of our adversary." No eloquence, no wisdom, no knowledge of psychology, no clearness of thinking, no simplicity of stating, no depth of feeling will avail to deliver a seeking soul unless we have first met the

enemy on our knees. Men are "taken captive by him at his will" (2 Tim. 2:26, KJV). Do we believe it? Have we felt it and faced it? If so, then we shall know that the victory on Calvary and the efficacy of the blood of the Son of God, believed and pleaded in prayer, are the only things that will make him give way and enable us to pluck the prey out of his mighty hand. Only so shall we cause men to repent toward God.

If there be no devil, then preaching, teaching, persuasion, and warning will be sufficient to deliver. But seeing that men are deceived and held captive by a subtle being, only God can save. He has appointed prayer on man's part as the way of deliverance, and has for some wonderful reason decreed that our cooperation in the conflict is necessary. He has, moreover, provided us with weapons other than carnal, whereby we may pull down the strongholds of Satan in the hearts and minds of men.

I pass to the second idea presented for our understanding of the nature of true repentance.

2) *To turn them to God.* The terms of the Gospel as preached by the Apostle Paul, he tells us in another place, are "repentance toward God and faith toward our Lord Jesus Christ" (Acts 20:21). Here, however, we need to emphasize one point—repentance toward God.

The modern version of "repentance" is outwardly very like the original—a change of mind—but inwardly as wide asunder as the poles. Of what avail would repentance have been to the prodigal unless he had repented toward his father? There is a so-called conviction of sin preached today which produces mere repentance. Sin is described as being beneath the dignity of human nature. Such is not the work *we* are called upon to do. We have nothing to do with the dignity of human nature, though much with its depravity. I shall in another chapter speak of how to set about the task. My present object is to make us realize that "all is not gold that glitters," that repentance is not necessarily repentance toward God, and that our work is not to make men break off their sins but to bring them to God, who waits to deliver. Satan cares not how earnestly we repent, if only we repent not "toward God." Turning men from the power of Satan means, above all things in these days, from the power of his sanctimonious counterfeits and the deceivings of self-righteousness.

### The Task: The Conscience Purified

. . . that they may receive forgiveness of sins . . . (Acts 26:18)

So far our commission has been but negative. The awakened, enlightened, and converted soul is not yet free, not yet saved, not yet a child of God, though very near it. There is still other and more important work to be done. We are commissioned to cause men to receive forgiveness of sins.

It is not decision for Christ that we are commissioned to preach, but *a faith that takes us to Him* as poor, sinful, selfish rebels, to receive at His hand mercy, grace, and pardon. This humbles, sweetens, and transfigures.

The deeper the sense of it, the more refined the soul becomes—chastened and changed into His likeness.

And yet our work is not merely to preach and teach its necessity, but *by faith and prayer* we are commissioned *to cause men to receive*. The difficulty in heathen lands is immense. As we have already seen, with no knowledge or thought even of a personal God there can be no sense of sin against Him; and so the conception of pardon, involving as it does the breaking of a Father's heart, as well as His laws, and meaning also the tender forgiveness of the sinner as well as of his sins, is entirely foreign and unintelligible to heathen minds.

## The Task: The Affections Renewed

. . . that they may receive . . . an inheritance among those who are sanctified by faith in Me. (Acts 26:18)

We come now to the last clause of our commission. Here is the real and final objective: *the new birth*—a radical change divinely wrought. It is a change of heart, likes and dislikes, purpose, mind, and will. The man must be made a new creature in Christ Jesus; and it is this that we are commissioned to cause men to receive. Note well that it is a receiving, a gift, a bestowal, a miracle inwrought as much as the pardon of sins. The gift of God is eternal life. "I will give you a new heart and put a new spirit within you" (Ezek. 36:26). We must never rest until we have reached this goal and secured this objective. We are the instruments that God uses for the accomplishment of this task.

## THE DYNAMIC OF A COMMISSION

The awakening of the prodigal, the enlightening of his eyes as he came to himself, his repentance in coming back to his father, the kiss of forgiveness, were all means to an end; they were blessed steps to the final objective of being clothed, fed, satisfied, and happy in his father's home.

Let us stand back awhile so as to get a perspective and *look at our wonderful commission.* If we have been forgiven and know it, if we have been made new creatures in Christ Jesus, then *we,* and not angels, are commissioned to minister this same salvation unto men and to witness of all these things which Jesus our Savior has revealed to us. Hallelujah!

CHAPTER 2
# Diagnosis of Man: The Desires

Because the sentence against an evil work is not executed speedily, therefore the heart of the sons of men is fully set in them to do evil. (Eccl. 8:11)

It was said of one of the great spiritual leaders of last century: "He now began to study human nature as it is, rather than as delineated in books. He discovered the necessity of knowing man in his general character, his weakness, depravity, and capabilities; of acquainting himself especially with the vulnerable points in the sinner's heart and the varied modes of address and modifications of personal feeling by which he might lay hold on the most powerful human passions and prejudices. He became a man of bold and successful experiment in human nature and ceased to estimate all preaching, and indeed all ministerial labor, except as it produced saving effects."

In this and the following chapters I propose to deal with the diagnosis of the human heart.

Difficult as our task in a heathen land may be, it can and must be accomplished. I used to fancy that the study was almost impossible to a foreign missionary. However deep an experience he might have of sin, yet being entirely unacquainted with the darkness and ramifications of superstition, it appeared to me impossible for him to be sufficiently informed for his task. Subsequently, however, I saw that God has given to us a perfect diagnosis in the pages of divine revelation. Hence our business, though not despising a study of the human heart in the natural, is to give ourselves to a diligent understanding of all that the Great Physician has diagnosed.

Here we can learn what is the material upon which we have to work; what are the strongholds we have to capture; what is the work we have to do; where and how to attack; what is the real condition of mind, heart, will, and conscience. These are the things that we need to know, and know them we must, if our work is to be other than merely beating the air, aiming at everything and hitting nothing.

The first task in St. Paul's commission was the awakening of the desires of men to the true, the imperishable, and the divine. Before setting ourselves to that task, we will consider in the present chapter their natural state in the unregenerate man, and more especially their attitude God-ward.

The doctrine of man as given us in the pages of Holy Scripture presents us with a very wide field of inquiry. I would urge every young missionary to make a careful study of this important theme.

The Word of God, in depicting the state of men's natural desires and affections, presents us with a terrible description. Men are said to be lovers of darkness (John 3:19), lovers of pleasure (2 Tim. 3:4), lovers of self (2 Tim. 3:2), lovers of money (1 Tim. 6:10), lovers of praise (John 12:43). The heart of man is said to be "deceitful above all things, and desperately wicked" (Jer. 17:9), unchangeable (Jer. 13:23), untrustworthy (Prov. 28:26), set to do evil (Eccl. 8:11), full of iniquity (Mark 7:21–22).

Now the Holy Ghost has declared that the "heart is deceitful above all things, and desperately wicked; who can know it?" (Jer. 17:9). It will not, therefore, profit us at all to make inquiries of the unregenerate heart itself, though it will help us much to listen to the verdict of those who have been renewed and changed into the image of Christ. They and they only can give an unbiased judgment of their original state. And yet it will profit most of all to turn to our textbook, the Word of God, if we would learn unerringly of the true condition of man's desires.

## Men Do Not Desire God

...they did not like to retain God in their knowledge.... (Rom. 1:28)

In seeking to turn men to Christ, let us start with this terrible fact. Whatever else men desire, whether of good or evil, they do not desire God; men are not seeking after Him.

God has planted within us a capacity for knowing Him, the instinct that should surely feel after Him, that it might find Him. But alas! alas! men seek Him not. That instinct has been paralyzed; the desires of the human heart have been poisoned at their very source. Let us not suppose that mere teaching or enlightening of the understanding will meet the case. By no means. Deep down in the human heart there is a rebellion and hatred of God. Men desire not Him. They hate to retain Him in their knowledge; there is not one that seeks after Him—no, not one.

Our own enlightened hearts, remembering the folly and shame of our unregenerate state, will bear witness to the truth of this sinister diagnosis. Men may desire peace, deliverance, and many other excellent things, but the verdict of the "true and faithful witness" stands: "There is none who understands; there is none who seeks after God" (Rom. 3:11).

There is to me no more convincing evidence of the depravity of human nature than this hatred of God. A missionary who gives much of her time to working amongst young men attending one of the higher schools in this country tells me with what avidity they devour and digest anything of German philosophy which seems to prove that God is non-existent.

For this remarkable fact in human nature there must be some terrible cause. One would naturally have supposed that men would delight in so beautiful a conception as the Fatherhood of God. If it is not true, it ought to be. If we cannot believe it, we ought to want to believe it. But alas! no. There is a bitter, blatant opposition to God in the human heart; and it is most bitter in the most educated.

## Men Do Not Desire Holiness

Depart from us, for we do not desire the knowledge of Your ways. Who is the Almighty that we should serve Him? And what profit do we have if we pray to Him? (Job 21:14-15)

Men love sin. Here is another terrible fact. Men do not desire a knowledge of the ways of God. They may not love all sin. There are many uncomfortable and unpleasant iniquities that we would all gladly be rid of; but it is true that men do not desire or love holiness of heart by nature. It is true that they are enslaved, but they are willing to have it so. The diagnosis in Romans 7:22, "I delight in the law of God according to the inward man," is not that of the unregenerate soul. Here again our own experience will corroborate the truth of this statement. If there is one sad and terrible fact in my own experience that I could be more positive of than another, it is that I loved sin, loved it with all my heart. I did not desire a knowledge of God's ways; my desires and affections were poisoned and corrupt.

Again and again I have appealed to heathen audiences; and they acknowledge it to be true, that the drunkard loves his drink, the profligate his lust, the worldling his money, the vain woman her vanity, the proud man his pride. These things are pleasant and sweet to the taste of the unregenerate man.

> In evil long I took delight,
> Unawed by shame or fear,
> Till a new object met my sight;
> And stopped my wild career.

At certain seasons of the year, in certain districts of Japan, one meets thousands of men and women visiting celebrated shrines in pilgrim garb. To a spectator from other lands, such a sight as this appears to indicate intense devotion and religious zeal. Again and again I have made inquiries, only to learn that these visits have no moral or spiritual significance whatever. "Prosperity in business, health to the body, peace to the home," an almost universal formula of prayer sums up the whole matter. If we add the following of custom, the excitement of a little outing, the whole "mess of pottage" strongly flavored with superstition, we have exhausted the motives that take these poor souls on their spring pilgrimages.

It matters not what the business may be—extortionate money-lending or the white slave traffic—prayer for its success is all in order. I have heard a native preacher graphically describe two suppliants at the temple: one, a poor woman praying for the deliverance of her profligate son from the harpy, whose "guests are in the depths of hell"; the other standing alongside of her, the proprietor of a "house . . . on the way to hell, descending to the chambers of death," supplicating the same god for prosperity in his vile business (Prov. 9:18, 7:27). The audience greeted the preacher's remarks with roars of laughter.

There seems to be a strange delusion largely obtaining in certain circles that the heathen are overwhelmed with a sense of sin. This is, of course, utterly ridiculous. Questioned on this point, educated converts have said that the consciousness of sin came to them only after they had become disciples of Jesus and had attained a personal spiritual experience.

Men have come to me desiring to become Christians. Inquiry as to their reasons has elicited the reply that they wanted "to be saved from sin." I remember one thus apparently in earnest. He was the victim of a violent temper and desired to be delivered; but further questioning showed that he had not the least intention or desire to forsake his other and more comfortable iniquities. He merely wanted to make a convenience of God. Similarly, a few weeks since, another came desiring to be a Christian, that he might become a respectable sinner instead of a drunken one! To have done with "all sin" was, alas! by no means to his liking, and so he went empty away.

"Christ for Japan" but never "Japan for Christ" might be written as an epigrammatic slogan over a good deal of the Christianity in this country. As with the nation, so it is with the individual.

### Men Do Not Desire Control
We will not have this Man to reign over us. (Luke 19:14)

Men hate divine authority. They hate a holy God and a divine Master. Not long since, in a country town, a most earnest idolater came to see me. After a long conversation, I faced him with this fact. In brazen fashion, he owned the truth. He said, "I love gods of my own making. I hate the God you preach—a just and holy God; my gods let me do what I like; yours does not." In other words, he would not have this Man to reign over him.

The pages of divine revelation boldly declare that man is a rebel, alienated from the life of God by wicked works—"enemies in your minds"—his desires and affections prostituted and defiled. If what I say is not so, then I have no gospel. It is no gospel to tell men that God merely loves good people and those that seek Him. There is not even *news* in that. The *new* thing and the *good* thing of God's message is that He loves sinners; He died for rebels; He waits to show mercy on the most open-handed sinner alive. This is news indeed and good beyond all reckoning.

Perhaps an instance, not from heathendom, but of one brought up amid all the civilizing environment of Christian England, may corroborate the truth. Caroline Fry, the author of *Christ Our Example,* a great saint and winner of souls, in speaking of her own conversion, tells of the revelation that came to her own heart of her true state before God.

The first real prayer she ever offered, the petition that opened the gate of Heaven to her soul, is deeply interesting and yet amazing in its honest confession of open rebellion and hatred of God. Possessed of beauty, position, wealth, and friends, she found them all hollow enough, and in utter misery of spirit she sought God. This is how she prayed, and this was the prayer that prevailed: "O God, if Thou art a God, I do not love Thee, I do not want Thee; I do not believe that there is any happiness in Thee; but I am miserable as I am. Give me what I do not seek, give me what I do not want. If Thou canst, make me happy. I am miserable as I am; I am tired of this world; if there is anything better, give it to me."

This was a true and honest declaration of the heart of man in its attitude toward God. That prayer prevailed because the petitioner took the position that God gave her. She told Him the truth; and that is all that God asks. "State your case, that you may be acquitted" (Isa. 43:26). "Only acknowledge your iniquity, that you have transgressed against the Lord your God . . . " (Jer. 3:13).

## Men Do Not Desire Christ as Savior

But you are not willing to come to Me that you may have life. (John 5:40)

How often I wanted to gather your children together, as a hen gathers her chicks under her wings, but you were not willing! (Matt. 23:37)

By nature, men do not want Christ. "When we see Him, there is no beauty that we should desire Him" (Isa. 53:2). Here is another appalling fact, and it is perhaps the most amazing of all.

Men's hearts are just the same today. So says the Book, and so records experience. Time has not changed the "unruly wills and affections of sinful men." Men will not come to Christ that they may have life. They still pass Him by on the other side, or at best render Him only a lip service. Let but His claims be pressed upon us, of a wholehearted surrender and service, and fierce, unrelenting opposition bursts out in flame, not nominally against Him, but against those who bring His message and His demands; as the Master Himself has said, "He who receives you receives Me, and he who receives Me receives Him who sent Me" (Matt. 10:40).

Some years ago, when at home, I had an experience that forcibly reminded me how sadly true is this unwillingness of men to come to Christ. I was dining with one well-known in the literary world in London one evening. When the two ladies had gone to the drawing room and we were left alone, the conversation turned to matters of religion. After a good many general remarks, my host turned to me and said, as nearly as I can remember, "Well, I think I may say that I accept the New Testament as true and believe all the facts of the life of Christ as told therein; but His life, teaching, and death have no more effect upon me than a fairy tale. A striking play at the theater moves me much more; and yet I feel sure that if I could but realize that God loved me personally, and if the facts of Christ's suffering and death were more to me than mere historic incidents, I would give my life to Him and serve Him at whatever cost."

I replied, "Your statement is deeply interesting, but does it not prove to your own mind the truth of Christ's words: 'Unless one is born again, he cannot see (that is, experience, feel, understand) the kingdom of God,' which is 'righteousness and peace and joy in the Holy Spirit' (John 3:3, Rom. 14:17). If you could feel and appreciate the love of God to you, and the power and efficacy of Christ's passion, with your own natural heart, you would not need to be born again. The fact, as admitted by yourself, that you cannot feel these things is established; and surely thereby you stand condemned. All that God asks of you is to come to Him just as you are, as a little child confessing your need, impotence, and unbelief. He will assuredly see to it that your need is met. He does not expect you to feel or realize anything until you are born from above. He has promised that He, not you, will take away this heart of stone, so that you shall feel and experience and be moved at His love and mercy and grace. Could any way be easier or more plain?"

Half vexed, half disappointed, he closed the conversation and turned to other themes. In my heart there echoed, "But you are not willing to come to Me that you may have life" (John 5:40). Any way but that; any step but the step down; any cry but the cry, "God be merciful to me a sinner!" (Luke 18:13).

As these four fearful facts fasten themselves upon our heart, that men by nature desire not God, love sin, hate authority, and refuse a Savior, the depravity of the human heart will be to us no theological fancy or religious fiction. It will drive us to our knees, to our Bibles, and out into the high places of the city to rescue the perishing.

CHAPTER 3

# Diagnosis of Man: The Understanding

Their foolish hearts were darkened. Professing to be wise, they became fools . . . (Rom. 1:21-22)

Every intent of the thoughts of his heart was only evil continually. (Gen. 6:5)

"Can anyone show me the way?"

It was the last cry, repeated again and again, heard by men as they went over the top. They left him dying in No-man's Land; and after talking over the day's experiences, they remembered it and wondered what it means.

"Did any of you tell him?" a Christian man among them asked.

"No, no," they said, "We didn't understand; we didn't know what he meant."

They didn't know, they didn't understand, though born and brought up in the so-called Christian land of England. Their understanding was darkened. What, then, may we expect of heathendom? We expect and find a darkness veritably Egyptian.

Although the desires of the soul may have in some degree been extricated from the slough into which they have sunk, and have caught a faint glimpse of an object which alone can satisfy the craving of the soul, the work is only begun; and we have to enlighten the understanding before there can be the exercise of any intelligent faith unto salvation.

I write here of the four great fundamentals of religion of which the heart is by nature ignorant: the existence of God; His gift to men; man's state before Him; and his way back to Him. Entire ignorance of these elementary and yet vital facts must be recognized by us and kept so vividly before our heart that we shall use every effort to find the way of enlightenment through study, prayer, inquiry, and every other means in our power.

## Ignorance of God

. . . the world through wisdom did not know God . . . (1 Cor. 1:21)

In so-called Christian lands, there is almost always a mental acknowledgment of the existence of God. This knowledge in an awakened heart at once produces conviction. Conscience has material on which to work. We can immediately use it as a lever to move the will and the heart of the penitent. In heathendom, there is nothing; only a darkness that may be felt, shrouding the soul even when awakened to its sense of danger and need. More convincing than any theory or explanation on my part will be the personal witness to these things. I quote a pathetic and deeply interesting experience of one who, once a heathen, is now a devoted preacher of the Cross. He writes thus:

> It was when I was ten years of age that for the first time I began to realize the fact of death. I remember quite well waking in the middle of the night and sitting up in bed. I began to think of death. I saw in imagination my body in the coffin, lying dead; I saw myself buried. It was so dark. I could not cry, though my young mind was agonized beyond all endurance. The thought that came to my heart was that the only one able to help must be some supernatural being, and I began to think about the gods. I counted them up one after the other; but they were almost numberless . . . I sought who he was, or what I could do; but I was dead in earnest, and I wanted someone to help me, and so I cried aloud, "Help me, O God; I am so helpless!" At length, tired, I fell asleep. On going to

school the next day I asked my teacher who the god was that I worshipped. He said he was one of the ancient heroes, a great man who was long since dead and buried. Oh! the disappointment when I realized that I was only praying for help to one who was himself dead and buried. I knew that I needed more than a dead man to help me. So the days went on into months and years. I was still in darkness. Whenever I was alone I would think and think by myself, but it was oh! so hopelessly dark.

My father used to talk to us about "heaven," as he was a disciple of Confucius, so I used to go out into the garden and look up into the sky, and thought, if I cried to the heavens, to the blue sky, is it possible that they will answer? It was all so empty, the blue sky.

Yes, that is all that centuries of natural religion can do for the soul; they could not bring the awakened heart to an understanding of the very first and elementary lesson of true religion, namely, the existence of a living God in Heaven. The heathen know not God.

There is, however, a gleam of light. Following my usual habit, I am always making inquiries of those who once were heathen as to their conception of God in their unenlightened days. I rarely find anything to encourage me, and yet at times I meet with souls in whom there seems to remain a vague, faint, uneffaced idea of a higher

Being. True, it is so vague, and so faint, that it never seems to appear to their own consciousness except in times of personal danger or under the enlightening rays of a gospel sermon. It is like the altar in the city of Athens erected to the unknown god. Amid all the labyrinth of darkness and superstition it may at least in some cases still be found; and yet I would hasten to add that, in Japan at any rate, the discovery is rare indeed. And yet, sadly true as this is, I have been amazed to see how God in His sovereign grace can enlighten a heathen heart with any human agency. To me this is pathetic in the extreme, for Scripture makes it abundantly plain that God's gracious design is to use man in carrying out His purpose of salvation. But alas! so backward and unwilling is the Church to accept this glorious responsibility, that God oft-times, through the Word alone or through dreams and visions, has to reveal Himself to heathen souls.

I cannot forbear again calling as witness for our encouragement the testimony of one thus enlightened from above. Imprisoned for murder, he served his life sentence (twenty-five years) of penal servitude and is now preaching the Gospel. After speaking of his desperate condition in jail, he proceeds:

> Under such conditions body and heart were completely overwhelmed. Then at that time I was unexpectedly and badly disgraced over an affair of which I really knew nothing. I burnt with furious rage and was almost driven mad.

I began to ponder how to clear my disgrace. I was too incensed to sleep that night, and the fire of indignation for my accuser burnt higher and higher.

At that time, mysteriously, a thought rose in my heart that if there be a God who is omnipotent and omniscient in the universe, and who surely has power to know all that is in our hearts, He should know and judge rightly the matter of yesterday. Oh surely He should! I had done no wrong. Well, I would commit this matter into His hands.

This thought came to me like a vision or dream; but it was very clear, and immediately my heart was stilled and I fell into a sound sleep. On the following morning when I awoke, I felt that the last night's malice had disappeared like a cloud; and on the other hand, the thought, "God knows everything, and I should commit myself into His hands," was very vital.

Next I thought I should try to read a Testament, to know something about God. It was in this way that the first stirrings of religious faith began in me. I began to read St. Matthew, line upon line, page by page, and I came on the pages that contain the Sermon on the Mount. Every word and every line struck me to the point.

After that, I got through as far as the wonderful words in chapter 11:28: "Come to Me, all you who labor and are heavy laden, and I will give you rest." When I came in contact with this Gospel I was so glad that I jumped up and cried, "This is the Book in which I trust!" giving myself up to its teaching.

Oh! I have read many books to get peace and joy in vain, and at last, when thirty-three years of age, I found a real faith. Oh! how sweet it was to read the Bible. I read, too, St. Mark 2:17: "Those who are well have no need of a physician, but those who are sick. I did not come to call the righteous, but sinners, to repentance." And through these words I was brought definitely to repentance and conversion, humbly asking of Christ forgiveness of my sins.

Though God in some cases may use such means as our witness here speaks of, yet His purpose is to use human lips and lives. Hence, I return to *our* task that we are called upon to accomplish.

In other and more heathen lands than Japan, I am well aware that the consciousness of the existence of a Supreme Being is less effaced than in countries where Buddhism, that supreme masterpiece of Satan, has almost entirely obliterated a consciousness of God. The more intellectual have thus been deceived more egregiously than the lower races. The darkness is in some respects more profound and more awful. But in either case, the ignorance of God is for all practical purposes paramount.

As a natural consequence of all this, there is another fact of which the human soul is oblivious, namely, God's claim. Obviously, when the existence of God is unknown, His claims upon us as Creator, Master, Father, and Judge are unintelligible. There are all sorts of substitutes, the so-called obligation of utilitarianism, the claims of the state, and what not; but God is not in all the thoughts of men. These blessed, tender, holy associations in the mind of the man who know and loves God, are not.

> Oh! the love that sought me,
> Oh! the Blood that bought me,
> Oh! the grace that brought me to the fold,
> Wondrous grace that brought me to the fold.

Constraining, binding, holding, impelling the redeemed soul to willing duty and happy service are wholly unknown. There is, moreover, no fear of God before their eyes. "The ox knows its owner and the donkey its master's crib; but Israel does not know, My people do not consider" (Isa. 1:3).

I do not know any subject on which there is less light than upon the sense of responsibility to God. The revolt of man has been so absolute, the determination to be his own master, the desire to be independent of all control, are so stubborn and of such long standing, that the idea of our yielding unfeigned obedience to the God of heaven seems almost unintelligible.

Coupled with this ignorance of our responsibility to God there is naturally an ignorance of judgment to come.

I have dealt with thousands of souls in my missionary life, but I have seldom met any who in the first days of their inquiry for salvation had any real sense of judgment to come. So absolutely has the prince of this world blinded his servants as to the issues of things.

"I listened and heard, but they do not speak aright. No man repented of his wickedness, saying, 'What have I done?' Everyone turned to his own course, as the horse rushes into the battle. Even the stork in the heavens knows her appointed times; and the turtledove, the swift, and the swallow observe the time of their coming. But My people do not know the judgment of the Lord" (Jer. 8:6–7).

## Ignorance of God's Gift

If you knew the gift of God . . . you would have asked. (John 4:10)

This is a necessary corollary of the ignorance of God's existence. How can men know God as the great Giver if they know not that He IS? And yet here is one of the great fundamentals of the Gospel. God cannot help giving, any more than the sun can help shining. If we will not let Him give us the best, i.e., spiritual gifts, He will at any rate shower upon us (the evil and the good alike) temporal blessings.

There are certain fundamental principles of religion about which the heart is naturally deceived. Strange as it may appear, there seems to be a tendency to be utterly blind to certain obvious and fundamental facts. It is interesting to note that the Holy Ghost in speaking of them precedes their statement with words such as, "Do not be deceived," as for example, "Do not be deceived, God is not mocked; for whatever a man sows, that he will also reap" (Gal. 6:7). One of the most striking instances of this is in reference to God as giver: "Do not be deceived, my beloved brethren. Every good gift and every perfect gift is from above, and comes down from the Father of lights, with whom there is no variation or shadow of turning" (James 1:16–17).

If men are thus ignorant of so simple and obvious a matter, doubly ignorant are they of God's spiritual giving. They may comprehend His Creatorship, His justice, and His power, but that He has a gift to bestow upon the sons of men, yea, and upon the rebellious also, they cannot understand or believe! So darkened have their hearts become. Do let us be convinced of this! Only so shall we set ourselves to enlighten men's minds on this vital theme. And yet we must be persuaded that it is an ignorance of the heart rather than of the mind. It is almost impossible for human nature to comprehend that God desires to give to the unthankful, the unworthy, the unlovely, and the evil. Human nature is so debased that it can only conceive of giving to those we love, or at any rate to those who are grateful, to the good, and to those who have some claim upon us through ties of relationship. This conception is so firmly rooted in the heart, that the beneficence, the benevolence, the compassion, and pity of God toward the ugly, the repulsive, the wicked, and the ungrateful is entirely alien to our natural understanding.

The ignorance of the heart in this particular is common to every unregenerate soul, whether nominally Christian or heathen. But it is deeply important for the young missionary as far as possible to project himself into the consciousness of the heathen mind in the matter of ignorance. From personal experience, I would say that as missionaries it is almost impossible for us to rid ourselves of the idea that the people to whom we are talking have not even an elementary notion of God's existence, His goodness, and His power; but we must extricate ourselves from this delusion if we are to succeed as light-bearers in heathen lands. Otherwise, we shall be talking above the heads and entirely outside the hearts of those we seek to win.

### Ignorance of Man's True Condition

[You] do not know that you are wretched, miserable, poor, blind, and naked. (Rev. 3:17)

The unregenerate heart, whether in Christian or heathen lands, is entirely incapable of knowing its own state before God by nature. A man may be able to think through the most difficult problems of philosophy, science, politics or finance, but unaided he is unable to diagnose his own spiritual state before God.

Our third task then will be to enlighten him here.

When I first came to Japan, now many years ago, I used to observe in the town in which I lived and worked a poor beggar in tatters and filth, looking supremely pleased with himself and his wretchedness as he went on his daily rounds of asking alms. Making inquiries, I found him to be a poor imbecile who was obsessed with the conviction that he was the Emperor of Japan. He was wretched, and miserable, and poor, and dirty, and imbecile, yet entirely ignorant withal of his state. My mind instinctively turned to the moral darkness of the human heart, as given in Revelation 3:17: "[You] do not know . . . " Yes, the mind and understanding of the unregenerate are darkened indeed.

In heathendom, vile profligacy is naively compatible with the most earnest devotion. In dealing with men, I have found nothing more bewildering and paralyzing than this ignorance of their condition. Sin seems to have no meaning whatever beyond the breaking of their country's laws. Again and again I have turned away sick at heart at the absolute and utter lack of sense of sin. The darkness is such as may be felt. It is, generally speaking, only when sin has conceived and brought forth its brood of suffering, misery, and shame that men feel something of the horror of iniquity, and even then not a horror of guilt against a holy God.

The ignorance of sin is the natural outcome of ignorance of God. The further ignorance of need is due to ignorance of God's gift and goodness. "If you knew the gift of God," said the Savior to the poor Samaritan woman. The heathen have never heard of the "promised rest," the "living water," "the divine power," and "eternal life," and so they but vaguely understand that they are weary, thirsty, impotent, and perishing. Let them but get a sight of ease of heart, the water that Christ gives, the liberty that can make them free indeed, and a salvation from the wrath to come, and at once the reality of their correlative need takes shape and poignancy enough.

The particular point that I would seek to emphasize here is that, however keen a sense the heathen may have of the evil effects of sin, or even of its moral iniquity as judged by utilitarian standards, their sense of guilt in the presence of a holy God is absolutely non-existent. They are hopelessly in the dark. To enlighten them here is the work of the Holy Ghost, and Him alone, though we are the instruments that He designs to use.

## Ignorance of the Way

The way of peace they have not known. (Rom. 3:17)

If you had known, even you, especially in this your day . . . But now they are hidden from your eyes. (Luke 19:42)

More disastrous even than all other ignorances is the darkness that hides from the soul the way of mercy, grace, and peace. In dealing with men that have become conscious of their need, their sin, and their alienation from God, interrogating them as to how to return unto the Shepherd of their souls, I am constantly amazed at their replies, even in the case of those who are reading and studying the Word of God.

"Repent," "do the best you can," "try to be good," "pray," "study Christianity," "join the church," "be baptized," are some of the answers to this all-important query, "What must I do to be saved?" Like the eunuch in his chariot, who, earnest, devout, believing in God, perusing the Scriptures, yea, reading the very words that reveal the way of Life, yet could not understand, the natural man knows not the way of redemption, vicarious sacrifice, forgiveness through the shed Blood of the Son of God.

Though in a sense we know all these things as more or less obvious facts, I am seeking in these pages to impress more deeply on the minds and hearts of my younger brethren in the missionary ministry how intense and real is the darkness that enshrouds the heathen world. Again I repeat it, unless we feel these things, we shall be robbed of the strength, determination, and the heavenly wisdom needed in the conflict. Only as we realize them shall we seek to equip ourselves for our task and study both the Word of God and the ways of men in order to enlighten them unto salvation.

Men know not God, nor that He is a giver; they know not their own state before Him, nor their way back to Him. They are "alienated from the life of God, because of the ignorance that is in them, because of the hardening of their heart" (Eph. 4:18).

CHAPTER 4

# Diagnosis of Man: The Will

The proudest heart that ever beat
Has been subdued in me;
The wildest will that ever rose,
To scorn Thy friends and aid Thy foes,
Was quelled, O Lord, by Thee.
Thy will, O Lord, not mine, be done,
I would be ever Thine;
To sing Thy praise, Incarnate Word,
My Savior Christ, my God, my Lord,
Thy Cross shall be my sign.

*—lines found in the Bible of one who had been an infidel*

I have before me as I write, a volume recording the testimonies of all sorts and conditions of men saved from heathenism in Japan. The first part of each life story is a record of enslaved wills. It is one long catalogue of sin, failure, and despair. Again and again, though having no sense of sin as a Christian understands it, yet awakened to a sense of misery through the cruel results of disordered desires, reaping an abundant harvest through the sowing of lust, hatred, and every evil passion, they tell the story of one long, defeated struggle of the soul; they repeat one long, pitiful cry, "Who will deliver me from this body of death?" (Rom. 7:24).

Our present chapter will deal then with the enslaved will, speaking more particularly of its four-fold bondage to Prejudice, Passion, Pride, and Fear. There is, however, another factor that I would first desire to emphasize. Behind all mere secondary causes stands the one great origin of evil—The Devil. Divine revelation makes it abundantly plain that men are "taken captive by him to do his will" (2 Tim. 2:26). Whatever means he may employ to imprison and enchain, he is the author of our bondage. Realizing this, we shall give ourselves to prayer and supplication; for we are dealing with forces that we cannot touch save by the throne of God.

Some years ago, an ex-Buddhist priest came into our meetings. After hearing the message not more than two or three times, he sought the Savior and was found of Him. (He is now a Salvation Army officer.) The change in his life was very marked and inclined his old mother to accompany him to the meetings. This she did for some weeks. I have never seen a more hopeless product of heathendom, darker or more superstitious than that old soul. Nothing ever penetrated her mind. She seemed unable to grasp the simplest idea; even after months of hearing the Gospel. I think we all gave her up in despair. She seemed so irrecoverably a captive.

There was with us at that time a very devoted servant of God from England. Hearing of the case, she wrote home asking for persistent and believing prayer on behalf of this old woman. Scarcely a month had elapsed from the commencement of the intercession before, in a most remarkable way, she was set free from her chains. Like a flash the light penetrated her darkened understanding, and like a little child she sought for pardon and deliverance.

### The Bondage of Prejudice

If you had known, even you, especially in this your day . . . But now they are hidden from your eyes. (Luke 19:42)

They hated Me without a cause. (John 15:25)

Prejudice is more than ignorance. If ignorance be likened to prison walls, prejudice is reinforced concrete. Many a soul, if only freed from prejudice, would at once be saved, but, alas! they are fast bound in its misery and iron. I have been amazed in listening to the testimonies of converts in our own Mission Hall, who in almost every case tell of their bitter hatred of Christianity (though knowing absolutely nothing whatever about it), on account of their blind, unreasoning and utterly unintelligent prejudice, which can only be likened to prison walls, through which there is neither entrance nor exit.

How to meet prejudice and ignorance I shall not have time or space to deal with in another chapter, and so I here make one or two observations. I have noticed that it is often necessary to let distressed souls sink deeper into their distress before they are ready to forsake their prejudice and turn to God for relief. Some years ago, a young man now in heaven had come into our Mission Hall, there to hear for the first time the good news of salvation. He was neither interested nor impressed. After the lapse of several months he found himself in great trouble and embarrassment. He called to mind the message he had heard and determined to seek comfort in religion. But his utterly unreasonable prejudice against Christianity, about which he knew nothing, though it had opened his eyes to the way of deliverance, made him turn to Buddhism for help. Finding this a broken reed, he again sank into despair, and shortly afterward meditated and even attempted suicide. It was not till then that he was constrained to cast his prejudice to the winds and turn to the despised and hated Nazarene for the salvation which he so soon and abundantly obtained.

I have observed after a long experience the means most effective in breaking open prison houses of prejudice is "love from a pure heart" (1 Tim. 1:5). The Holy Ghost flowing out in streams of love and joy from the heart of some humble Christian has proved sufficient to undermine the walls of prejudice which have so long incarcerated the heathen soul.

Perhaps none are so imprisoned by prejudice as Jews. And yet none are more susceptible to the love of Christ when manifested in one of His children. Elsewhere I have referred to the conversion of a young Hebrew in the city where I have been laboring. His prejudice against Christianity was bitter and intense. He utterly refused either to talk of spiritual things or look at the Scriptures. His remarkable conversion was due to the vision of Christ as revealed in and through Christians he met.

Someone has observed that the only Bible the non-Christian ever reads is a book some five-odd feet in length bound in human skin. It is the perusal of this book alone that will shatter the walls of prejudice and set the prisoner free.

### Bondage to Passion

... you do not do the things that you wish. (Gal. 5:17)

No one comes to the Father except through Me. (John 14:6)

If prejudice and ignorance are the prison-houses of the soul, evil passions are its chains. Everywhere we find men fettered by evil appetites. At first willing captives, imagining that silken cords are easily broken, young men and women gladly give themselves to their lust, only to discover before long that when they would be free, their slavery is complete.

In dealing with such, it is important to distinguish this form of bondage from other and more hopeless cases. In reality the slavery to evil passions is more easily removed than any other, if only we know how to bring them to Christ just as they are. A striking instance will illustrate. While recently in England and staying at one of the military centers, I sought to help in one of the huts erected for the soldiers. One Sunday evening I had the privilege of listening to the story of its leader. His case so exactly illustrates my point both as to the bondage of sin and also as to the way of deliverance, that I here relate it.

Born of drunken parents, himself a drunkard in his early teens, often in jail, unable to read or write, a hopeless bit of flotsam on the wave of London life, he was one day, through the kind offices of his poor wife, skillfully piloted outside the zone of public houses and found himself listening to an open-air service. One of the speakers, coming up from behind, lovingly put his hand on his shoulder and urged him to seek the Savior.

Half in despair, half in anger, he retorted, "What is the good of asking me to do that when I am nearly always drunk? While the whisky is pouring down my throat I hate myself and know what a fool I am, but I cannot help it. How can I be a Christian?"

Opening his Bible at Romans 5:6, the preacher read to this poor, unlettered slave, "For when we were still without strength, in due time Christ died for the ungodly." He bade him observe the connection, "without strength" and "ungodly." "The reason," said he, "you have no strength and are a slave of the drink is that you are without God. If you can get back to Him, He will see to the drink craving for you. You have not to break off your sins and then come to Christ, but come just as you are. Christ has died for you just as you are."

The poor fellow, utterly amazed, could scarce take in news so good; but hastening home, far into the night he cried to God just as he was, pleading Romans 5:6, which he had succeeded in memorizing. To him it proved the talisman to victory, a very passport to heaven. His chains fell off; he was freed from that hour; and many is the poor drunkard that God has allowed him to point to Christ since then.

## Bondage to Pride

Unless you are converted and become as little children, you will by no means enter the kingdom of heaven. (Matt. 18:3)

Far more desperate than the bondage to prejudice or passion is the enslavement of the will to pride. Here, too, in seeking to lead men to Christ it is most important to bear this in mind. Only so shall we be able to point them to deliverance and so strike at their fetters. The forming of resolutions and the exercise of the will cannot bring relief; that will only make them drift into deeper bondage. The Master has said it: "No one comes to the Father except through Me." Only Christ can deliver; and our business is to bring them to Christ.

After patient inquiry, and having discovered that the man we are seeking to help is in bondage to pride of heart rather than evil passions and appetites, and having further observed that he is awakened to a real sense of need, our one task must be to insist that he humble himself as a little child and bring his pride of heart to the Savior. In doing this, however, we shall discover that there is somewhere a weak spot in the strong man's armor. He is certain to know it, and it is there we must press the attack.

Earnest prayer and a constant insistence on this one point will certainly meet with success.

## Bondage to Fear

And whoever does not bear his cross and come after Me cannot be My disciple. (Luke 14:27)

Here is another of Christ's inexorable "cannots." I have often seen men, though free from prejudice and pride, still in bondage to sin because enslaved by yet another chain—fear. The Devil has no more effective means than this to enslave his captives. Fear hath torment. There is no such thing as fear in heaven; it is forged only on the anvils of hell.

I have been amazed at the strange, unaccountable power that idolatry has over the hearts of men even after all belief in it has disappeared.

Fear is evident in two distinct forms: 1) superstition, or fear of evil consequences resulting from change of faith; and 2) fear of man. These, I say, are separate and distinct.

The first is extraordinarily deep-seated. Even in the minds of Christians there are still very evident traces thereof. Failure in business and want of success in various undertakings, sickness and bereavement, etc., are attributed by heathen to the anger of the spirits of the ancestors because they are not worshipped. Again and again it is possible to discover, even in the minds of ill-instructed Christians, a lurking suspicion that this is so. In the minds of the heathen, it is a mighty and entrenched force. The will to break loose from these strange superstitions at times seems almost impossible. When we meet these difficult cases, prayer and the Word of God are the only means available for breaking their wretched fetters. We need to remember they are forged in hell and are some of the Devil's most powerful means to enslave the wills of men.

A few days since, I met with one, a professing Christian, who consistently fails in all he undertakes. On the very verge of success, he suddenly tumbles; God seems to blow on every venture. On my explaining to his wife that the reason was plain enough, namely, his refusal to seek first the Kingdom of God in order that all these things may be added, she at once replied, "I am sure that is the truth. I tell him so, but he is inclined to believe what his relations say, namely, that his failure is due to the insults he offers to his ancestors in not doing them worship." It is in vain that I tell him heathen may succeed by seeking their material interest first, but God will never let Christians thus dishonor Him. He will hinder their undertakings every time till they learn at last His blessed law—first His Kingdom, then all things added.

The second kind of fear is equally paralyzing. It is the species we in Christian lands are most familiar with—the fear of man. Truly it "brings a snare" (Prov. 29:25). It is just as strong in central China, Africa, and Japan as it is in London society. It is one of the soul's most deadly foes. Thousands are in hell today because they were "fearful." They, as well as the "unbelieving, abominable, murderers, sexually immoral, sorcerers, idolaters, and all liars . . . have their part in the lake which burns with fire and brimstone" (Rev. 21:8).

Failure in diagnosing is fatal here. In nine cases out of ten, the seeker will conceal the truth; it is one of the last things that he is willing to acknowledge. Again and again I have wondered why the professed convert makes no progress, until I have discovered that through fear of man he is unwilling to confess Christ openly before others.

I have found it absolutely necessary, as in the homeland, to urge that essential condition, "with the mouth confession is made to salvation" (Rom. 10:10). I think the Asiatic is by nature more of a moral coward than the Westerner. He hates to lose face. The fear of man is a very powerful influence with him. Individualism is to him a new thing. To act apart from his family and parents in such matters as changing his religion is a very serious offense against society and the customs of his people. Unless we are on the lookout for this obstacle, we may get on the wrong track and be dealing with difficulties that do not exist, wondering all the time why the seeker makes no progress in his quest for salvation.

In conclusion, I would add a word of caution. In all cases of dealing with the *wills* of men, we need above all things to beware of argument and controversy. That great soul-winner, Charles Finney, continually insisted that the difficulty lay in the will and not in the mind. We shall meet with all sorts and conditions of men: the utterly indifferent (Luke 12:17–21), the self-righteous (Luke 18:18–30), the genuine self-righteous inquirer (John 3), the wicked and godless (Luke 19:1–10), the casuist (Matt. 22:23–33), the political religionist (Matt. 22:15–22), the self-deceived enthusiast (Luke 9:57–62), the unawakened but thirsty sinner (John 4), the convicted sinner (John 8:1–10), the death-bed penitent (Luke 23:39–43), etc., etc.

All of these will, of course, need different treatment; but whoever or whatever they may be, let us keep ever before us that the trouble is largely that of an unsurrendered will. Hence argument and controversy are both fruitless and fatal. "True doubt," it has been observed, "always causes excruciating pain." When we come across anyone doubting in such fashion (alas! I fear they are very rare), we can indeed deal very tenderly with them and seek to answer their difficulties; but, as a rule, so-called intellectual doubt is only a cloak for sin, or at least for an unwillingness to yield to the Savior.

Let our main purpose be to bring men to Christ, provided that they are awakened, enlightened, and convicted. Seek to impress on the penitent again and again that if he will only return to God through Christ just as he is, his will, be it vacillating or strong, be it enslaved or prejudiced, can be at once renewed and made perfectly whole. Christ is the only remedy—Christ, and Christ alone.

> Yea, thro' life, death, thro' sorrow and thro' sinning,
> He shall suffice me, for He hath sufficed;
> Christ is the end, for Christ was the beginning;
> Christ the beginning, for the end is Christ.

CHAPTER 5

# Ministry and Witness

He who wins souls is wise. (Prov. 11:30)

Be diligent to present yourself approved to God, a worker who does not need to be ashamed, rightly dividing the word of truth. (2 Tim. 2:15)

I have already pointed out that one of the main purposes of these pages is to show that God calls us to reap as well as to plow and sow. I am further seeking to show that in heathen lands we can lead souls to Christ far more swiftly than is generally deemed possible. With this aim in view, I suggest four important considerations.

## A Sincere Belief in the Possibility of Immediate Harvest

Do you not say, "There are still four months and then comes the harvest"? Behold, I say to you, lift up your eyes and look at the fields, for they are already white for harvest! . . . I sent you to reap that for which you have not labored . . . (John 4:35, 38)

Many a young missionary accustomed to the joys of harvest in his home church or mission hall reaches his station on the foreign field, only to be told almost at once, "You cannot expect that sort of thing in heathen lands. Without a long period of instruction, it is impossible to expect that a soul can pass from darkness to light." Alas! his keen ardor is thereby surely if insensibly cooled, and a dull, non-expectant spirit is at once engendered in his mind. This is fatal. There must be a driving conviction in the heart that it is possible for one entirely ignorant of the Gospel to be saved within a few hours of his first hearing the message if only he has been prepared by the Spirit of God and his heart has passed through the crucible of suffering, sorrow, or sin.

The instances in my own experience are so many that it is difficult to make a selection. Perhaps it may be best to choose one instance from those who have put their experiences into writing and thus can speak for themselves. It is the testimony of a man who is now a much-used evangelist, filled indeed with the Holy Ghost. He says:

Previous to the night on which I was saved I do not remember ever having heard anything of Christianity in my life, except on one occasion when I drifted casually into a Salvation Army meeting at Osaka, and even there I could hardly say that I attended the meeting; I merely stood on the outside and listened for a few minutes. It made no impression on me whatever. I could not tell you anything of what I heard.

The date of my conversion was on the 21st of September, nearly six years ago. I entered the J.E.B. tent erected where the new Mission Hall now stands. Mr. W was preaching on 'What we believe, and Why.' I remember it as though it were yesterday. 1) The existence of a living, loving, almighty God. 2) The existence of a living, fearful, nearly almighty devil. 3) That God loves men and will hear their prayer. 4) That men love sin in their heart and commit it in their lives. 5) There is a judgment to come. 6) God has provided a way of salvation and escape through Jesus Christ.

I was deeply convicted of my need. I had no sense of sin against God as I now understand it. I cannot put into words exactly, in what my sense of sin consisted—whether against self, against others, or against God—but I had a strange sense of sin. It was vague and indefinite, but very real. I believed that night that God could help me. I stayed to the after-meeting, and though, of course, I had not what I now have—a clear understanding of Christ's person and atoning work—yet in my desperate need I put my confidence in Him as He was declared to me that night, and for His sake I asked God to receive and save me.

The change wrought in me was immediate and astonishing. As I look back on it now, I am lost in wonder, love and praise. The next morning, I found myself to be a new man. All the old fetters were broken, and I was free.

While recently on furlough, at a drawing room missionary meeting I was emphasizing the necessity of thus expecting an immediate harvest even in heathen lands. There was in the audience a very devoted and well-known missionary from China. She was at the time interested in a class of Chinese who were working a laundry not far from Liverpool. These men had been attending a Bible class at her home some little time, and she had been seeking to instruct them in the teaching and principles of the Gospel. She returned home determined by faith and prayer to put the matter to the test. At her very next meeting, she had the joy of leading one, if not two or three, to the Savior. She wrote to me to tell of her joy. That was some years ago. Only a few days since, passing through this city on her way to China, she recalled the incident, and told me how bright was her Chinese laundry man convert whom she had brought to Christ.

All, of course, will not be thus led. Many will move much more slowly; but if only our faith and expectation, our prayer and our presentation of the Message were more definite, concise, and insistent, many a soul would find the way to peace and be saved of the Lord as swiftly as the dying thief on the cross or the heathen jailer at Philippi.

## An Understanding of the Minimum of Truth Required to Lead a Soul to Christ

. . . rightly dividing the word of truth. (2 Tim. 2:15)

It is obvious that no man can believe intelligently unto salvation without understanding a certain amount of truth. The important question is, how much? As I have already observed, the mark of a great preacher in heathendom is his ability to discern how much content he needs to put into the mind of the hearer before he can use it as a lever to move his heart, will, and conscience. This is an urgent essential. It is easy to bewilder an inquirer and discourage him by a superfluity of discourse, giving him theological stones for spiritual bread.

I remember many years ago a young man, then a bank clerk, now the pastor of a large church, had been timidly coming every night to hear the Gospel. He always slipped away before the meeting was closed. One night, however, I waylaid him and invited him to my home. I sought at once to lead him to the Savior, being satisfied that he was an awakened and sufficiently enlightened soul. I remember very distinctly his looking up and saying to me, "Do you mean to say that is all I have to do?"

"Yes," I said, "that is all for the present."

He seemed astonished that it was not necessary to understand all the truths of Christianity before he could become a Christian. He at once trusted the Savior and was born of God. He continued in the way of the Lord, finally himself receiving a call to the ministry.

Our need then, to put it briefly, is the ability to eliminate for the time being all truth not absolutely needed to bring the Light of Life to a convicted heart.

To put the matter in something of an epigram: Our task is not to put the fire out, but to pull men out of the fire. Blessed be God! The Lord Jesus at His advent will quench the conflagration of iniquity and sin and bring in everlasting righteousness and rule with a rod of iron. In the present dispensation, He commissions us to "take out of them a people for His name" from every kingdom, nation, and tongue (Japan, thank God, is yielding its quota); and when the Lord of Glory appears, He will have a glorious company that no man can number prepared to be "rulers over cities," to "judge the world," to "judge angels," and with Him to govern the earth (Acts 15:14, 1 Cor. 6:2–3).

I repeat it—the truth we must know and proclaim must be saving truth, the old-fashioned Gospel of salvation from sin. Until we are deeply persuaded that this and this alone is the world's need, we shall never be winners of souls.

## A Faith in, a Study of, and a Knowledge of How to Use the Word of God

Receive with meekness the implanted word, which is able to save your souls. (James 1:21)

The story is told of a missionary returning to Africa from furlough and taking with him a number of trifling presents for his people in the interior. Amongst other things, he took some small mirrors; one of these he gave to an old lady, who was immensely pleased with her new-found treasure until she-realized that it was reflecting her own features. She, of course, had never seen a mirror before. As soon as the poor soul realized what it was doing, seeing that she had no idea how withered and ugly she was, she proceeded to smash the mirror to pieces with the utmost indignation. She did not like to know the truth; like the proverbial ostrich, she preferred to hide her head in the sand.

The parable is plain! The Word of God is the looking glass, and unlike that of Alice in Wonderland, it shows us the truth as to the state of our own heart, as well as the love and grace of God. Perhaps of all things required for soul-winning, the study of the Scriptures is the most important.

Many a missionary has himself had a painful experience of sin, and therefore knows how to deal with a stricken conscience; but in no case, I suppose, has he had any experience of the darkness of superstition. It is impossible for him to project himself experimentally into a heathen consciousness. It is most important, therefore, that he have some source of information and means of diagnosis and discernment other than mere conjecture or an academic study of natural religions if he wishes to penetrate the labyrinth of a heathen mind.

It is very easy to be deceived by the one we are seeking to lead, unless we have a light that never fails; but God, who searches the hearts and knows the thoughts of men, has given to us in the pages to His Word all the psychology we need to know in order to convict, wound, bind up and heal, enlighten and deliver.

First of all, there must be an absolute *belief* in the plenary inspiration of Holy Scripture. Personally, in my own experience (and it is by no means small), I have never yet met a man wise to win souls who has rejected the plenary inspiration of Holy Writ. I know of many men with striking personality, dominant will, and rich, intellectual training, who in their ministry and intercourse with men have influenced and attracted them to themselves and their opinions, only to discover after they have been removed, a sure relapse either into worldly ways or open indifference to religion.

Every soul-winner will unhesitatingly believe that the Word of God presents us with an infallible diagnosis of man's lost estate and need and equally declares to us an infallible panacea for his misery and sin.

Above all things, then, we need to study the Book and accept its descriptions and diagnoses as unalterably true. In spite of all academic vaporings to the contrary, do we believe that man is guilty (Rom. 3:19), dead (Eph. 2:1), at enmity with God (Rom. 8:7), blind (Eph. 4:18), helpless (Rom. 5:6), a lover of sin (2 Thess. 2:12), in bondage to Satan (2 Tim. 2:25–26), by nature, depraved (Rom. 5:19), and in danger of everlasting destruction from the presence of the Lord (2 Thess. 1:8–9)? If we do not know and feel these things, how shall we ever set ourselves for man's deliverance?

Secondly, the soul-winner will need to *study* the Word in this particular connection. The knowledge of men and things, an acquaintance with the human heart, are also vital, but a close study of the Scriptures will alone make us successful in dealing with men. Only so shall we be able to use it in order to convict and wound, bind up and heal.

Thirdly, the soul-winner must be *able to use* the Word of God. Mere faith in and knowledge of the Book is insufficient.

Perhaps an illustration will make my meaning plain. Some years ago, I was privileged in having a share in the conversion of a young Jew, then residing here in the Far East. To all intents and purposes, he was a heathen. He had no knowledge of any Christian truth whatever. Seeking for something to satisfy his soul, he got entangled for a time in the meshes of Theosophy. He tells the story of his deliverance in part as follows:

It was at this point, after I had had the fellowship with Mr. W and his household for some little time, and when I had a vague and shadowy conception of the main truth of the Gospel, that God in His wisdom saw fit to divert my thoughts to entirely different channels. I made the acquaintance of a young man some few years my senior and found that he was interested in psychology, a subject to which I myself had been greatly drawn, and from this fact there resulted a friendship between us, from which in turn resulted a mutual exchange of ideas. My new-found friend proved to be a Theosophist, and it was not long ere I found myself ardently perusing the various books that he put in my possession—books that tended to lead me very far from the Gospel of Christ . . .

When, therefore, I next visited my friend Mr. W, I set myself out to advance certain arguments adduced by Theosophists, arguments which directly opposed certain doctrines held by followers of Christ and which, on the surface, seemed very plausible. Mr. W allowed me to hold forth without any interruption for some considerable time, and then, without making any remark, he stretched out his hand for his Bible (which was never far from his side), and with a smile proceeded to open the same. He then, to my utter amazement, read passage after passage, which directly anticipated the various arguments and theories that I had put forward. As he read of those who in the last days would come, "having a form of godliness I but denying its power," I could not but feel how well these words applied to Theosophy, which so strenuously opposed the idea of a Personal Deity whilst extolling moral rectitude (2 Tim. 3:5).

As I sat and listened to words of Scripture written hundreds of years back, and which yet anticipated a condition of things prevalent in our own days, there came to me the deep conviction that I must not lightly set aside the Book from which the words were taken, did I sincerely desire to know the Truth. [He had steadfastly refused up till now even to have a Bible in his possession. - P.W.] I had not hesitated to read Theosophical literature, and likewise should I not hesitate to read that which was claimed to be the Word of God? I told my good friend Mr. W of what was passing through my mind, adding, however, that I still believed the New Testament to be a human and not a divine compilation.

His answer to this latter remark was very simple and very helpful. He read to me Hebrews 4:12: "For the word of God is . . . sharper than any two-edged sword," etc., and then added the following illustration:

"Let us suppose that I come to you with a naked sword in my hand, stating that it was exceedingly sharp and requesting your examination of it. You, however, assert that I am holding, not a sword, but a walking stick, and all my appeals to your intelligence and power of sight fail to alter your opinion to the contrary. To convince you of your error I would thereupon ask you to catch hold of it, and the wounds thus inflicted would speedily disillusion you."

To apply the illustration was not difficult. From this hour, I set myself to read the New Testament, and it was not long ere I indeed realized that I was dealing with a sword and found myself grievously wounded, so that my spirit found no rest night or day.

It will, I think, be no digression at this point to add a warning. One of the greatest foes that we have to face in the mission field is the so-called Higher Criticism. I could fill pages with illustrations of this statement did space and occasion permit. Not only is its desolating influence seen among the pastors of the various churches, but alas! its effect upon the laity is evident on all hands. I can only entreat most earnestly my younger brethren in the ministry, if they want to be winners of souls, to touch it not. As I have remarked, I could call many witnesses, but one must suffice. I shall therefore stand aside and let him give his damning evidence. Mr. Kanamori is not only well-known among the churches of Japan, but his name is a household word throughout the length and breadth of the land, as for some years he held an important post in the Home Office. He speaks as follows:

> Well do I remember the Dedication Day, a beautiful, clear Sabbath morning, January 30th, 1876, when the famous Kumamoto Band was formed. There were just forty of us who that morning marched up the hill called Hanaoka (the Hill of Flowers). After the reading of the Scriptures and the singing of the missionary hymn, "From Greenland's icy mountains"—all in English, of course, as we had nothing then in our own language—I, a boy of eighteen years, offered the prayer of dedication by which we gave ourselves to God and His service. Our closing hymn was, "Jesus, I my cross have taken, All to leave and follow Thee," and that had a very literal meaning to us, for till that time each one had had quite high ambitions. For my part I had planned to become a great shipbuilder, foreseeing what great need of ships our Island Empire was to have. Others had large plans of high official position, well based on their good family connections. So we were truly giving up all for the Master.
>
> And the sacrifice was not long delayed, for persecutions began as soon as our families heard of our acts, and they were very severe.

One boy was shut up at home for a hundred days; others were severely treated in various ways. For my part, at the end of my trials I was disinherited and driven from home with literally nothing but the clothes on my back and two books in my hands. These were my Bible and a copy of *Pilgrim's Progress.* Laughing, I told my friends that I still had these two weapons with which to fight the devil.

But God had prepared us a refuge even before we knew it. The famous Joseph Niishima had returned from America and was then just opening his school at Kyoto. To that school we went, and thirteen of us entered the Theological Department. Three years later I went from there and opened the church work in Okayama, where I was pastor for seven years. Then my beloved teacher, Dr. Niishima, failing in health, I was called to help him; and from then till his death some four years later I was with him continually, helping as his caretaker and as his substitute in the school.

Then began my time of wandering, for I came in touch with all phases of modern thought, so-called New Theology, and German Higher Criticism, several books of which I translated and published, to the great injury of my people. Upon me must chiefly rest the blame for the theological errors of Japan, for I stoutly strove for them by voice and pen, even in the secular press. So bitter was the controversy that some of my old friends announced that they could never again shake hands with me, but I went proudly on until my faith was entirely undermined and overthrown.

Radical Criticism had robbed me of my Bible, and New Thought of my Savior; and with no faith in my heart, there was left no message on my lips. As soon as my revered teacher went home to glory, I also left the school and took to secular matters. As the new Constitution had but just been granted by our Emperor, and the political parties were struggling for the mastery, I plunged in as a social reformer for several years. Then for fifteen years I was a governmental official in the Home Office, and my duties were to teach the people thrift and practical economics. In this capacity I traveled all over the land many times, addressing thousands daily. The crowds were always too great for any building and were held in the open, and the people hung on my words with profound interest and attention.

From the worldly standpoint, at this time my life was a great success. With ample income, official position, and name widely known, my popularity was such that the people would almost force their gifts upon me. But mentally these years were my darkest, without peace or genuine satisfaction in anything. And at the zenith of this apparent prosperity, God laid His hand upon me with a sudden and terrible blow, taking from me my dear wife.

I was as one dazed for a time, not knowing which way to look for comfort. But suddenly in my own family the light began to shine, for the simple faith of my children assumed as certain truth that "dear mamma" (as they called her with the English word) was surely gone to God. Their firm faith and childish talk were used of God to bring me back to the truth. And when I came back, it was to my original faith in my Savior and God's Word. No more do I feed my soul on a "Bible full of bones and no meat," but on the "strong meat" and "finest of wheat." No more do I talk of Jesus as a "God-filled Man," but with doubting Thomas I humbly claim Him as "my Lord and my God." And thus, again I have the soul-satisfying message of "the glorious gospel" of the Son of God. Apart from such faith no such message can exist.

## The Study of the Human Heart

Also He has put eternity in their hearts . . . (Eccl. 3:11)

The story is told of the Marechale once walking through a large library in Paris accompanied by a university professor. She expressed her pity for the poor students who had to read and study so many volumes, observing that her own studies were limited to two. On his inquiring what they might be, she replied, "The Word of God and the human heart," adding, "I am therefore never lonely."

We too are not likely to succeed unless we make a study of the human heart and its ways in actual life as well as the Word of God. May I very strongly urge this upon my younger missionary brethren?

I have made it a constant practice to inquire carefully of Christians and young converts as to their experiences. What was the first thing that impressed them, interested them, or awakened them? What was their first point of contact with the Gospel? What made them first desire to be Christians? What was their experience at the time of their first trusting Christ? What was the Word that God first spoke to their souls? I make a further point of eliciting as far as possible information as to their former prejudices, superstitions, ignorance, and sins.

This method of constant observation and inquiry both from Christians and inquirers is most helpful to themselves. It enables them to focus their thoughts, making what before may have been dim and hazy, luminous and distinct; it helps them to understand the miracle of their own conversion, the goodness of God and His grace, as well as the sinfulness of their heart. It furthermore reveals possible defects in their spiritual life and experience.

In the second place, as I have already observed, it is essential to our own success. From information thus gained, we know how to reach the hearts of others. "We should have the Bible in one hand and the map of the human mind in the other and know how to use the truth for the salvation of men." From information gleaned through inquiry, we know how to do this. I have thereby been enabled to observe in my own preaching what sermons and addresses have reached the hearts of the people, what illustrations and what passages from the Word have been most effective.

It has another and greater importance still. Through observation and inquiry, we are able to acquire most valuable material for reaching the consciences of men. When all else fails, personal testimony or the recital of such will awaken and convict. This is the Scriptural method. The Bible is full of personal testimonies, given in much detail and point. The stories of individual conversions are so many that they almost seem out of all proportion to the size of the sacred volume, dealing as it does with the whole scope of Divine Revelation.

Not long since, I had an experience that illustrates my point. While I was at home on furlough, I went to take a meeting at Glasgow and speak on missionary work. In the course of my address, I had occasion to tell the rather striking story of a poor drunkard. I told it in some detail, emphasizing the need of coming just as we are in honest confession and humble prayer. I am not certain that a mere recital of the conversion of the drunkard would have been effective. I took pains to record my observations of his conversion and repeated them in some detail, that his experience might thus be made of value to other storm-tossed souls.

A month or six weeks later, I received a letter from a poor old peddler, a slave to whisky. He had stumbled into the missionary meeting half drunk, but getting a little sober by the time I had reached the narration of the above story, he said to himself, "Well, if God can save a poor heathen drunkard as easily as that, He can surely save me." There and then he lifted up his heart to God in broken confession and believing prayer. The hand of God, which is not shortened, reached him as he sat in his pew and snapped his fetters in a moment.

His letter, which lies before me as I write but is too long to quote in full, contained a thank offering of one shilling, to be given "to the next poor drunkard in need" that I might meet.

I got and kept in touch with him and found that God at once began to use him amongst other drunkards. Only a few weeks had elapsed before he got twelve others to sign the pledge, two of whom he had been able to lead to the Savior.

Just before I left England, a year after his conversion, I was taking meetings at Birkenhead. At one of them, my old peddler friend, with Hallelujahs on his lips and a smile on his face, reintroduced himself to me, and told me of yet other trophies of the Cross won through his testimony and service. A little seed it was from far Japan, cast at random and carried by the wind (the Spirit) fifteen thousand miles into the soil of a poor old drunkard's heart in Scotland, there to bring forth a golden harvest.

These are the simple and yet strange means which God employs in the salvation of souls, that all the glory may be His.

CHAPTER 6
# The Commission

I became a minister according to the gift of the grace of God given to me by the effective working of His power. To me, who am less than the least of all the saints, this grace was given, that I should preach among the Gentiles the unsearchable riches of Christ, and to make all people see . . . (Eph. 3:7-9)

In the foregoing pages we have been considering the importance of diagnosis lest we drift into mere religious quackery, while in the preceding chapter I have endeavored to suggest four simple considerations that might help us in our task. In the present chapter, I want to continue the subject and present four very elementary principles as to the actual way of working.

There are other most important considerations, but in order to be as simple as possible, I shall confine my remarks to one suggestion under each of the following terms of our commission:
- How to awaken the soul
- How to enlighten the understanding
- How to turn the will from Satan unto God
- How to cause men to receive the gift of eternal life

## The Awakening of the Soul

From our own inventions vain, of fancied happiness
Draw us to Thyself again, and bid our wandering cease.

Before ever we seek to enlighten the mind or deliver from the power of evil, converting the will to God, our first task must be to awaken the soul. It seems almost unnecessary to point out that in attempting to do this we have to approach the heart by two avenues, or, to put it in other words, we have two things to accomplish, namely: l) to awaken a sense of need; 2) to produce conviction of guilt and sin.

No conversion can be real and satisfactory unless both are secured. But an important question arises as to which of these should be prior to the other. A mistake here may be a great hindrance. If we deal first with the sin, in some cases at any rate, before the sense of need is sufficiently developed, we shall most certainly frighten our quarry away and lose the one whom we are trying to win.

For our own instruction, it is necessary to know how depraved and rebellious and evil are the desires of the unregenerate heart, but in approaching the one we are seeking to lead, the better way is to produce a counter attraction and hold up the Water of Life till it sparkles before the eyes, thus creating a thirst and desire for true satisfaction. Then we can readily pass to the deeper question of sin and guilt.

I have been perfectly astonished how many souls have come to Christ (and as their subsequent life proves, the conversion is real and genuine) without any sense of sin at all. Here is a very remarkable case in point. The young man in question now has gone to his heavenly home, where he had a glorious entrance a few years after his conversion. He writes as follows:

> It was not long before I sank into depths of profligacy, but this evil way had no happiness for me. At last I began seriously to consider whether there was anything in life worth living for, and so at 10:30 on March 1st of this year [1909], I decided to commit suicide. I bought some poison, left the house where I was living, and made my way up to the mountains, there to take my life without being easily discovered. As I passed a graveyard on my way up, suddenly there flashed into my mind the words of Matthew 11:28, which I had but *once* seen on a screen in the J.E.B. Kobe Mission Hall. As I sat in the Hall, how well I remember saying to myself, "I am not laboring, and I am not heavy

laden; I have not use for that sort of religion." But now, as I was on my way to commit suicide, they came vividly before me . . . My mind was awakened, and I gave up all thoughts of death. I returned home, and at 4 p.m. the next day I went to the Mission Hall. There H-San welcomed me and unfolded to me the Truth. I stayed to the evening meeting, and as I listened I felt that the preacher was speaking every word at me and to no one else. After it was all over H-San and K-San helped me to pray and led me to the Savior, and there I found peace with God.

He came to Christ in the first instance realizing nothing but his deep need. Later, thank God, he learned his sin and the immensity of God's pardoning grace, as well as of His saving power.

A study of the way in which the Lord Jesus approached men and presented His Gospel to those that were sinners (I am not speaking of His way with Pharisees) both illustrates my point and makes it appear that He invariably appealed to the selfish instinct in the unregenerate rather than to the altruism, which by modern theologians is supposed to exist in the natural man, and which in present-day sermons forms almost the sole basis of appeal. Christ's appeal to the altruistic, when made at all, always seems to have been directed either to those in whom the Spirit of God had already begun His work, or also, as in the case of the young Ruler, to expose his self-deception, and thus show that in the unregenerate state, even of the best, there is no such thing as pure, unadulterated altruism at all.

In all the many conversions I have seen in Japan, I have never met one who came to Christ with other than a selfish motive. Thank God! when we have thus come, He can transfigure and so implant into our soul His own divine altruism that all subsequent appeals to the regenerate nature may be appeals to the highest and noblest traits of a sanctified character.

And yet here I would digress a little. It is possible to awaken souls by this appeal to altruism if rightly presented. The Lord Jesus made use of it; so may we, if we use it as He did.

It was John Wesley who said that the fundamental and distinguishing difference between all forms of Natural Religion on the one hand and Revealed Religion on the other is the doctrine of man. The former teaches that there are some good qualities in man and some bad (the only need therefore being to cultivate the virtues that the vices may thereby be displaced). Revealed Religion declares that man is totally depraved, and that even his supposed altruism is but selfishness after all.

If we bear this carefully in mind, we may yet use the weapon of altruistic appeal to awaken and convict.

No man lives unto himself. He either leaves a trail of misery and shame in his track, or an aftermath of blessing and peace. As we press this consideration upon the more thoughtful, an awakening sometimes follows.

Many a man living a dreamy, self-pleasing, indolent life, with no particular vices to his account, may be awakened by such a challenge. What is your life? What are its influences? Whom are you touching, reaching, moving, blessing, and filling with light and gladness? Is the world any better for your being in it? Who shall rise up and call you blessed? I must, however, sadly confess that in heathen lands seldom do such appeals reach the heart until it has been regenerated by the Spirit of God. Though to some self-satisfied, self-righteous Pharisee, it is conceivable that his poverty, nakedness, and shame may be so revealed, and thus he may awaken to his real need.

Before leaving this important theme, I might refer to an entirely different type of inquirer—I can hardly say seeker. I mean the scholastic youth who suffers from "swelled head." He delights in absolutely demonstrated proof that there is no such thing as a God that can be known. He loves to argue and prove to his own (if not other people's) satisfaction that poor missionaries are "back number."[2] And yet he often appears in the guise of an inquirer. He is, he would tell you, a searcher for truth and an honest doubter, who really wants to know and do. Beware of such. The young missionary will be dragged into fruitless controversy before he knows where he is. The only physic that will avail for this type of inquirer is large doses of Romans 1. Don't be afraid to hand it out. Rejection of God is followed by awful effects. In heathen lands you are safe in handling the terrible themes of that

---

2  Out of date, old-fashioned

chapter without kid gloves. Avoid crossing swords over the existence of God. Talk about sin. Press the battle to the gate. Here again the secret is the same. Get at the question of God through the conscience and the heart; and if light won't enter that way, it will never enter any other, or by any other means.

## The Enlightening of the Mind

"Let there be light," again command,
And light there in our hearts shall be;
We then through faith shall understand
Thy great, mysterious majesty:
And by the shining of Thy grace
Behold in Christ Thy glorious face.

Our next task is the enlightening of the awakened. How are we to proceed? How are we to instruct, for instance, on the subject of the existence, claims, and power of the living God? Here again we turn to the Great Exemplar. All His instruction, very much given in the form of parable, was always made to the understanding through the channel of the heart. For instance, in the story of the Prodigal Son (full of the deepest philosophy), where the main point is the existence, love, claims, and power of a living God, the simplest language is used; no attempt is made to prove anything. The strongest appeal is made to the conscience, will, and affections of the heart, thus carrying with it an unanswerable enlightenment and proof to the understanding.

The mere impartation of knowledge and instruction has no power to move to action; the forces that impel men to act are limited to four: Fear, Hope, Faith, and Love. In the ordinary affairs of life, all actions spring from one or more of these secret sources: *fear* of poverty, suffering, failure, or shame; *hope* for success, wealth, wisdom, and ease; *faith* in ourselves, friends, circumstances, and environment; *love,* gratitude, and sympathy—the highest motive of all—these are the secret forces in the mind that impel to action. And, of course, it is not otherwise in the still more vital matters of religion.

In Pascal's immortal words, "Le coeur a ses raisons que la raison ne connaît point," "The heart has reasons that reason knows nothing of." Dissertation on the existence of God, metaphysical disquisitions on His unity and creatorship, etc., are not an effective way of enlightening the darkened understanding if we want such enlightenment to bring conviction and conversion.

This is true in every particular. In seeking to enlighten the soul on any great theme of the Christian faith, it should always be done in language and thought, which will at the same time reach the conscience, will, and affections. Alas! it is here that there is so much failure. The Garden of Eden method, if I may be allowed the expression, still obtains. The fruit from the Tree of Knowledge is purveyed from all the theological gardens (perhaps I should say wildernesses) and handed again and again to hungry souls as though it were fresh clusters from the Tree of Life.

Alas! it proves to be but husks (Luke 15:16), wind (Hosea 12:1), and ashes (Isa. 44:20), and the awakened soul turns again to its slumbers. Whatever the theme—the existence of God, the immortality of the soul, the incarnation, the life, death, resurrection, or ascension of the Lord Jesus—see to it that its presentation is closely associated with an appeal to the conscience, will, and affections of the inquirer. Preaching that merely instructs and interests is only a darkening of the understanding, mere counsel of words without knowledge.

I am constantly coming across the melancholy results of the lecture-room type of homiletics. One who is now one of our most experienced and much-used workers had listened to that type of preaching for some years. It produced nothing but an incitement to argue, and it left neither desire, nor determination to turn to God. But coming accidentally into our Mission Hall one night, for the first time, as he says, he heard what reached his heart. He made haste to repent of his sins, turn to the Lord, and be saved; and with it, thank God, he learned the lesson of how to reach others like himself. Writing some time afterwards he says,

> In Kobe I went to work at a Dockyard Co. and testified daily to those who worked with me. While waiting for my employers to return in the luncheon hour, I used to give out tracts, though my companions jeered and called me "Yaso" (the name for Jesus used in derision) . . . I would never argue; I simply testified of my salvation.

Faith is not arguing; it is practical experience. One young man asked me whether the Bible was a revelation of God. I replied that it was, and that it showed the way of life. "That is pure superstition," said he, and left me. A few weeks later he became an earnest seeker for Salvation.

Yes! He had learned that it is impossible to be saved by syllogism and that cold logic will neither awaken, enlighten, or regenerate a dead soul.

## The Liberation of the Will

Jesus, mighty to renew,
Work in me to will and do;
Turn my nature's rapid tide,
Stem the torrent of my pride;
Stop the whirlwind of my will,
Speak and bid the sun stand still:
Now Thy love almighty show;
Make even me a creature new.

In the great commission given to St. Paul, the third task assigned him was to turn men from the power of Satan unto God, or in other words, to set men free from the Devil, who has taken them captive at his will.

Some years ago, a young man came to me with a desire to be a Christian. His mind, however, was full of all sorts of difficulties; he was sure of failure, he said; he was tied and bound and unable to get free. Our subsequent conversation ran as follows:

p.w.: Why don't you get alone with the Lord Jesus and tell Him what you have told me?
inq.: But perhaps I am a hypocrite.
p.w.: Well, tell Him that.
inq.: I am not quite certain that I am really in earnest.
p.w.: Why not tell Him that too?
inq.: But my will is so weak. I don't think I could hold out.
p.w.: That's something else you can tell Him.
inq.: But perhaps, etc., etc., etc.
p.w.: Well, you can tell Him that as well.
inq.: Do you mean that is all I have to do?
p.w.: Yes, that is all for the present. Go to Him exactly as you are; but whatever you do, tell Him the whole truth: all the bad things and weaknesses, and sins, all that you know. You can leave the good things about yourself alone. 'Put Me in remembrance; let us contend together; state your case, that you may be acquitted' (Isa. 43:26).

He left me rather dubious, I fancy, at so easy a way of deliverance. Some weeks passed, and I received the following letter:

I have done as you bade me, and now I know that you told me the truth. The questions I had are still unanswered; they are still there; but I recognize their fruitlessness now. They have lost their sting; they are like serpents whose fangs have been pulled. I don't know how I can thank you . . . I have seen the vision, and I have a faith which, as you said it would, has already led me through two trials which I would have run away from before. There are other things even more important which I cannot mention even to you. But what a blessing it is to have Someone to go to Who is big enough to understand and cure all our meannesses, if we will only tell Him the truth! I realize I have never been happy before in my life, and at the same time I don't think I have ever been so sincerely sad. You will understand the paradox. How can I ever thank you for introducing me to Him?

This theme is so vital that, at the risk of being wearisome, I will put the matter in yet a different setting. The liberation of the will is only another name for repentance. Now it is commonly represented that the forgiveness of sins and the gift of eternal life are bestowed of God, but that repentance is rather an act of the sinner himself. This is, of course in a measure true, and yet not altogether so. For repentance is as much a gift of the Ascended Christ as the forgiveness of sins or eternal life (Acts 5:31).

Here is a simple and wonderful secret in leading souls to Christ. We must insist that they come to Christ just as they are. Here is the difference between the Old and New

THE COMMISSION 87

Testaments. The Old was "Thou shalt" or "Thou shalt not." The will of the sinner had to do it all. In the New, it is "Christ received by faith" in place of the effort of our will. Christ does what we cannot. He says, "I will," and not, "Thou shalt." We have but to *will* to believe. We have but to declare that we may be justified. We have but to confess that we may be forgiven and set free.

Had the young ruler on hearing the Savior's drastic conditions but cried: "Lord, I came to Thee thinking that I needed a little more instruction in order to secure life eternal, but alas! I find that I cannot do what Thou dost bid. Now I know that it is a Divine Savior and not a moral instructor that I need. Now I know that my will is enslaved and I am powerless to obey, I can only cry, 'Save me, or I die.'" In a moment the blessed Savior would have granted repentance unto life, working in him to will and to do according to His good pleasure, as He did a few hours later to Zacchaeus, another ruler and another slave to his purse-strings, but one who, unlike the former, was not only a sinner but knew it.

## The Saving of the Soul

Aye unto them distributeth the Giver,
Sorrow and sanctity; and loves them still;
Grants them a power, and passion to deliver
Hearts from the prison-house and souls from hell.
—"*St. Paul*" *by F.W.H. Meyer*

There is but one thing that concerns us here in the present chapter, dealing as it does with the way to execute our commission. Just as we and not angels are commissioned to awaken, enlighten, and convert the souls of men, so are we called not merely to tell men of the salvation that is in Christ, but to cause them to receive. This is a fact so wonderful that I desire to focus our attention in the following sentences upon this one point.

Let us consider it closely. The calling to accomplish so extraordinary a work means, of course, that after patient inquiry and study of the case in hand, we must be able under the Spirit's guidance to apply the truth from the Word of God that will exactly meet the need of the seeker. But it means also much more than that. God has given to us the privilege of helping souls to believe, to lift them, so to speak, in the arms of faith and so help them into the Kingdom of Heaven. Perhaps I cannot do better than quote from the life of that remarkable man, John Smith, of last century, to whom I have referred already. His biographer says of him:

> It was with him a firm conviction that sin must be repented of by someone; and if sinners would not repent themselves, the people of God must repent on their behalf. It was therefore a settled principle with him to confess the sins of the people, and unless a preacher carried about with him a daily burden he is not likely to see many sinners converted to God. "It is possible," he said, "to believe for a penitent"; and in confirmation of this opinion he

has related instances in which, when he has been laboring to exert this faith of sympathy, actual faith has arisen correspondingly in the mind of the sinner, and the power of God and the joy of salvation have burst upon both as they simultaneously appropriated the atonement of Christ.

And again:

We are capable of acting upon men. A divine influence is connected with every Christian. God and Christ require it of us. We have power with God for them. Their state must be looked at with as much particularity as possible. The Atonement must be believed for them; the promises of the influence of the Holy Spirit must be seized and pleaded for them; their hardness, profanity, pride, and carelessness will give way.

This truth is so important, and the missing of it means eternal loss to ourselves and to others, that I quote from the life of another wonderful soul-winner, William Carvosso. His biographer says of him:

He saw in the strong, commanding light of faith Christ present, able, willing to save unto the uttermost. In no man's lips whom I have heard speak on matters of faith did it ever appear to me that the word "believe" meant so much as in his. When others said to the penitent "You must believe," the words often appeared without force and almost without meaning; but no sooner did he utter these or similar words than the wisdom of God was manifest, and Gospel truth spoken in simplicity frequently seemed like a lever that moved the world. Hence the multitude of captive souls that found almost instant liberty when they fell into his hands.

Some years since, I was able to obtain an interview with one of the most notorious criminals in this country. He had been condemned to death on three different counts. The circumstances of the murders—one of them a little child—were of the most revolting description. The man had been educated at a Mission School; his parents were both professing Christians, at first R.C.s, and subsequently members of the Episcopal Church.

I found him eagerly reading the Bible and other Christian books; I was allowed just thirty minutes in the presence of three warders, one of whom took down all that I said. I never saw him again after that, so that I am unable to say if he was found of the Lord. He asked me to see his father, which I did; and never has it been my lot to witness such unutterable grief and misery of spirit. On the day of his execution, he sent me his New Testament, which I still have in my possession.

I told the circumstances of the poor fellow and my visit to his cell to a fellow missionary, a woman of wonderful piety and power in prayer. I think that I shall never forget the agony of soul which she endured for that man for many days until he was actually beyond the need of any human help. She pleaded before God with strong crying and tears. If ever I meet him in heaven, it will be through the agonizing intercession of that saint.

Such is the Commission—a dynamic indeed to one who knows that it has been given to him of the Lord. Like St. Paul, he stands amazed that such an honor could ever be entrusted to him. It is a dynamic that sends us to our chamber, bows us in the dust, humbles our hearts, and stirs up to seek God and wait upon Him for the vision, the power, the tenderness of heart, and the wisdom that comes from above.

We cannot present to others the salvation of God as sufficient to satisfy the deepest longings unless we ourselves are drinking of the Living Water, abiding in the Promised Rest, standing fast in the Liberty wherewith Christ has made us free, and looking forward with joy to the Hope of Eternal Life ready to be revealed.

We cannot enlighten darkened souls, unless the light of His salvation and His presence are to us a living, bright reality.

We cannot offer Christ as an uttermost Savior from the bondage of every evil thing unless He has made us free indeed.

Above all, we cannot lift up other souls in the arms of faith unless our own hearts are at leisure from themselves to soothe and sympathize, and through faith in Jesus' name we find ourselves strong to meet the infirmities of the weak.

The failure to execute such a commission as this with power may well make us weep in secret places, and I am inclined to think that until the realization of our privileges, our opportunities, and our failure does take hold of us in some such fashion, we shall not be successful as fishers of men and ambassadors of the Most High, beseeching men to be reconciled to God.

CHAPTER 7

# The Sense of Need

The poor . . . the brokenhearted . . . the captives . . . the blind . . . those who are oppressed . . . (Luke 4:18)

In the preceding chapters, I have spoken somewhat of the method to be adopted in seeking to awaken, enlighten, and convert the soul. The task, however, is so difficult in a heathen land, and so important (one indeed to which a missionary cannot give too much thought) that I propose giving two more chapters to this theme. The first will be devoted to a consideration of the sense of need; the second, to that of sin.

To be an effective workman, the study of the avenues of approach to the human heart is absolutely vital. Until we have understood these, we shall certainly fail to effect an entrance; we need to understand the various means at our disposal and the various ways of approaching men. This we cannot do unless we learn from the pages of Divine Revelation. When we do understand, we shall not be disappointed at the failure of our first attempt; for we shall bear in in mind that if one avenue is blocked, we may try another and yet another, until we strike the point of least resistance, or in other words, the place where the Spirit of God has evidently prepared a place of entrance.

Now apart altogether from the subject of sin, there are four distinct, definite means of approach to the soul along the line of need. God has implanted in every man four wonderful instincts. They have been poisoned and perverted, but the Gospel reveals the poison and provides the remedy.

The first instinct is *a desire for rest, happiness, and joy*; the second for *power and dominion* over all that appears to us to be harmful and evil; the third for *light and assurance*; the fourth is *a desire for perpetuity of life*.

These desires are all divinely implanted instincts, and in seeking the salvation of the soul, while showing how depraved they have become, we need to present an object which in every case will meet and satisfy each of them to the full. They are, moreover, the four means used by our Blessed Lord Jesus Himself. They are the four motives to which He appealed; they speak to us of four aspects of salvation; they meet the four great needs of the human heart. They are applicable to every soul in every land in all time.

Christ is made unto us wisdom, righteousness, sanctification and redemption—or in other words, light and assurance; peace with God, and the peace of God; deliverance from sin and iniquity; and finally, eternal life—the redemption of our body as well as of our souls.

## The Desire for Rest

Come to Me, all you who labor and are heavy laden, and I will give you rest. (Matt. 11:28)

Christ offers, first of all, rest of soul. Such was the message that reached the heart of the woman that was a sinner (Luke 7 and Matt. 11). I do not know of any word in Scripture that has been more used in Japan to awaken sinners than this. We have seen it again and again. I should far exceed the limits of this chapter if I began even briefly to record the testimonies of those who have come under my own observation. Repeatedly men and women on the way to commit suicide have been arrested by this message: rest to the *conscience* from guilt; to the *heart* from sin; to the *will* from rebellion; to the *desires* from lust; and to the *body* from the results of evil; to the *mind* from care and to the *soul* from the fear of death. It is well to take each of them and by an illustration from life apply it to the hearer.

The real reason for unrest is, of course, the absence of anything abiding on which to repose. It is like a weary man preparing to rest on the couch, only to find it snatched from under him just as he is settling to repose. Such is the world; it provides naught abiding.

From experience, I have furthermore observed that trouble, sorrow, and care are schoolmasters to bring men to Christ. Not a sense of sin, but a desire for rest has often turned men toward heaven. Thank God, we have a salvation and a Savior that can meet this need, as well as take from the souls of men the sorrows of their iniquity and their transgression.

In presenting this blessed aspect of salvation, I have found it good to insist upon the Person of the Savior as much as upon the fact of His salvation. Though men know it not, their craving for a Person to love, sympathize, and help is one of the deepest instincts of the human heart; and it is this instinct that we need to awaken, enlighten, and satisfy.

May every young missionary know how to offer rest to the soul and so preach the Blessed Rest-Giver to men that He shall see of the travail and labor of His soul and be satisfied no less than the sinner himself who rests on the bosom of the Good Shepherd.

Closely akin to this longing in the human soul is the desire for joy. "But the water that I shall give him will become in him a fountain of water springing up into everlasting life" (John 4:14). Here the Lord Jesus presents an object to the soul, exactly adapted to meet this same need: *the desire for happiness and joy.*

God's purpose for man is his supreme happiness, perfect joy, and pleasure forevermore. This is a most blessed instinct; and God purposes to satisfy it. Man has devised all sorts of evil fancies to secure it for himself; and we, in seeking to snatch the poisoned cup from his lips, will succeed only by holding up to him the elixir of eternal life, namely, heavenly joy. There is no substitute for it. In the jail at Philippi, lacerated backs and bleeding limbs could not quench it. In amazement, the brutal jailer, as he beheld it, was soon a weeping penitent at the feet of those whom he had tormented. I may add that there is no pleasure in the Lord's service more exquisite than seeing it bubble up in the hearts of those who were once bowed down with care and hearing the lips that once kissed idol stones burst forth in songs of praise and gladness.

I have before me a large pile of letters from such. I cull a few quotations from some of them: "I am so full of joy that I scarce know where to begin . . . I am so happy that I sometimes think the joy is more than I can bear." And another: "I have never experienced such joy as I do today. I am amazed how wonderfully the Scriptures have opened up to me." And yet another: "I cannot keep still for joy. How is it possible that I could ever receive such a gift as this? I will ever cherish the love of Jesus in my heart."

Blessed as it is to see men and women full of great joy in the homelands, it cannot be compared with the sight in heathendom. To preach effectively the message of joy, we ourselves must find it springing up within our own hearts.

A few weeks ago, I was visiting the beautiful foreign-built residence of a Japanese. One of the inmates was a very earnest Christian. I inquired how she had been led to the Savior. She told me that when she was a school girl of about fifteen, the Rev. B. F. Buxton visited the town in which she lived. She attended his meeting, adding, "I understood not a word of what he was talking about, but the sight of his face, the joy of his countenance, so convicted me that I vowed I would never rest till I found the salvation of the Lord."

## The Desire for Power

And you shall know the truth, and the truth shall make you free . . . Therefore if the Son makes you free, you shall be free indeed. (John 8:32, 36)

Stand fast therefore in the liberty by which Christ has made us free, and do not be entangled again with a yoke of bondage. (Gal. 5:1)

There are many souls to whom the appeal of rest or joy is scarcely an appeal at all. Their difficulty and their need lie in an entirely different direction. To them the power of sin is the terrible reality. By that I do not mean guilt. This is particularly so in heathen lands. Except in rare cases where there has been a considerable degree of previous instruction, I think I have never come across a soul who has been overwhelmed with a sense of guilt and a need to be forgiven, in the early days of his inquiry. This is, of course, natural. Where there has been no knowledge of God, the sense of sin against His laws and the wounding of His heart must of necessity be almost impossible.

In so-called Christian lands, the case is far otherwise. Some years ago, I had the joy of leading an Englishman in this city to Christ. He was deeply moved and convicted of sin. The one cry of his heart was, "How can God ever forgive me? I have sinned so deeply against Him." The contrast between him and a heathen seeking salvation is very striking. In the latter case the cry is, "Who will deliver me from this body of death?" rather than, "God be merciful to me a sinner" (Romans 7:24, Luke 18:13).

I have observed that the sense of sinner-hood comes later. The soul moves backward, so to speak; he obtains deliverance, life, power, and victory, and then, as he is instructed in the things of the Kingdom, he learns the magnitude and depth of the mercy of God in pardoning his transgressions, as well as of His power in giving deliverance. Like the poor paralytic of old, he comes to the Savior for power, but the Lord says unto him, "Man, your sins are forgiven you" (Luke 5:20).

I do not wish to be misunderstood. We should endeavor by all means in our power to show from the beginning the greatness of guilt and the absolute necessity of pardon. Without this foundation there is nothing. It is all-essential. I can well imagine someone reading these pages interrupting me with an objection: "Surely, then, there is need for deeper instruction on the fundamentals of the Christian faith before we can urge a soul to believe?" To this I would say, "No!" a thousand times. I believe that the Lord Jesus comes to a soul just where he is, as did the Good Samaritan of old.

If I may say so, there are three distinct stages in the conviction of sin: 1) sin against ourselves; 2) sin against others; 3) sin against God. Owing to ignorance, the seeker may have arrived only at the lowest stage of all. He knows he is a poor drunkard, or a slave of lust; he knows nothing of sin against a holy God, and perhaps very little of the misery and hell he is causing to others. He knows only that he is a slave. Am I to wait till he is duly instructed on the immortality of the soul, the trinity of the Godhead, the holiness and justice of God, the incarnation, life, death, resurrection and ascension of the Lord, yes, or even a thorough sense of sin against God before I can urge him to be saved? God forbid! Salvation in the last analysis is not our apprehension of the truth, but a Divine bestowal, a gift, a miracle, a work of God. It is LIFE, and when that has been imparted, there will not only be movement upward and heavenward from within, but a blessed light and illumination on the immensity of God's pardoning grace as well as His deliverance.

Dr. Torrey tells the story of an attempt on the part of a number of agnostics to break up one of his meetings. Being advised of their presence in considerable numbers beforehand, he opened his service by asking all who had been saved from a life of sin and degradation through faith in Christ to rise to their feet. A large number responded. He then asked if there were any present who, having lived a dissolute life, had been suddenly converted into good and useful citizens by faith in the principles

# THE SENSE OF NEED

of agnosticism. If so, he requested them likewise to stand. There was no response except on the part of a colored man, who, however, turned out to be hopelessly drunk at the time.

Many a time have I used that illustration and challenged a heathen audience to produce a single instance in this vast city of 600,000 people of anyone enslaved to lust and liquor (yea, and even to despair) being suddenly transformed and delivered through faith in any form of heathenism whatever. It is remarkable that, though there are many authentic instances on record of healing through idol worship, in all the twenty-three years of my work I have never met with anyone delivered from sin thereby. My challenge is always unanswered.

This liberty is, of course, the very essence of the Gospel. "You shall call His name JESUS, for He will save His people from their sins" (Matt. 1:21). After all, peace and joy are rather the results and corollary of salvation from sin. We need above all things to be able to present an absolute and immediate salvation from sin to those who are bruised and bound.

Our presentation of this salvation must be definite and arresting. We must insist that it can be received in a moment. Let it always be presented through the words of Scripture, unfolded and explained, then illustrated from life, and finally fastened and clinched with the words of Scripture again which alone are able to make us wise unto salvation.

## The Desire for Light and Assurance

He who follows Me shall not walk in darkness. (John 8:12)

A study of the Lord's life, teaching, and miracles, especially as recorded by St. John, discloses the constant appeal He made to this instinct of the human heart. The desire to know, to be assured of the eternal verities of life and the hereafter lead many a distressed mind into the "forbidden ground" of spiritualism and psychic research, only to find will-o'-the-wisps leading to swamp and quagmire of eternal wretchedness and shame. To this desire we may well appeal. Christ is the Light as well as the Life of the world. He, and only He, can dispel the awful uncertainties as to the "unending dark" of future existence. Only He brings "life and immortality to light" (2 Tim. 1:10).

In seeking to awaken the sense of need, we may well use this powerful weapon. Deep down in the human heart is the longing for eternal life, strong and abiding, however much Buddhism has sought to smother it with its theory of Nirvana and the annihilation of personality.

Only today I received the following letter from a Buddhist priest who had been brought to Christ some three months ago when one of our missionaries went to open up work in a new country town. He has borne much persecution for Christ, being turned out of his home almost naked. He writes thus about his conversion:

> I have an uncle and aunt who are earnest Christians. When I was at school in Hiroshima, I

lived with them and for a year attended a Sunday School; but being the son of a Buddhist priest and myself intended for the priesthood, I was not allowed to attend further when I began to go to High School. The prospect of the priesthood pleased me well. I was deeply interested in philosophy; hence, unlike other young men of my own age, I was immensely taken up with pessimistic views of life. Buddhism, which is of course practically atheism and teaches the annihilation of personality, was a creed with which I was very satisfied, until some years later I met with an event which completely dissipated all my faith in such extreme views of "idealism."

I had a dear friend whom I loved better than anyone else in the world, better than a brother. He was suddenly taken ill, and within three hours was dead. This produced an extraordinary change in me; I lost all my interest in the study of philosophy. Every night I used to see my friend in my dreams. Could it be, I thought, that the friend I talked with but yesterday has now gone forever? Does he live no longer? I could not but believe that his spirit was still living somewhere. The more I thought of it, the more I was convinced that it must be so, and a deep longing to *know* possessed me. My study of Indian Buddhism provided no answer to my questionings. I had believed that Indian Buddhism was superior to any other system of religion or philosophy in the world, but now I lost all faith therein.

From that time onward, I lived in a realm of doubt. I then began to study the doctrines of the Shinshu sect, which professed to teach a future life. This, however, failed to satisfy me, and I turned then to another sect—Hogekyo, the teaching of which is perhaps the most profound of all Japanese Buddhist communities. None of these, however, could answer my question or satisfy the desire of my heart. The problem of life appeared as insoluble as ever, and death seemed the only solution.

I had the deepest sympathy with Fujimura Misao, the brilliant student who threw himself over the Kegon Waterfall. Like him, I meditated suicide again and again. The one thing that kept me from it, however, was the thought of, "After death—what?" Will death really end all the suffering of life? Is the death of the soul as certain as the death of the body? Whither goes the soul when separated from the body?

Ten years since the seed sown in my heart at Sunday School at last began to bear its fruit. I had thought that my entrance into the Buddhist priesthood had altogether choked the seed, but it was not so. The rain and sunshine at last brought it forth. My Buddhist training and philosophy was only a case of the winter before the spring; at last the springtime came. I can only praise God that by His infinite grace He brought the light into my soul, saved me from all my darkness and sin; my sorrow fled away, and on March 21 of this year, the sun rose in my soul, never more to set, and I was saved of the Lord.

Knowledge is peace as well as power. Men need to know the things that are freely given them of God ere they can be at peace in their own hearts on the one hand and have power to help lead men on the other.

## The Desire for Eternal Life

For God so loved the world that He gave His only begotten Son, that whoever believes in Him should not perish but have everlasting life. (John 3:16)

In representing desire for eternal life as one of the supreme desires of the human soul, I would add thereto the desire for salvation from fear of death and from the judgment to come.

I have grouped together these three things, as though their presentation to the heart constituted a single means of awakening the sinner to a sense of need. They are, however, as distinct in experimental conviction as in fact.

In Japan, and possibly in other heathen lands, the conception of a judgment to come is, I have discovered, vague and feeble in the extreme. The Buddhist representation of hell is so extravagantly crude that it has become by almost common consent to be regarded as a mere *deus ex machina* to scare people into the practice of virtue, with not even the semblance of truth behind it.

It may be urged, therefore, that from those who have no knowledge of a personal God and hence no sense of guilt, we can hardly expect to find any rational response to the doctrine of a judgment to come. To this I would reply that we are dealing not with ideas, but facts, not with men's perverted mentality, but with the statement of the Holy Ghost about the most awful and solemn of all realities. We can leave it to Him to convince of its truth and reasonableness. I beg, therefore, all my younger missionary brethren to use in faith and deep conviction the terrible words of Revelation 20:11–14 and 21:8. They will reach the heart; they will convict; and the terror of the Lord will turn men back to the Lord who is ready to forgive and who delights to pardon.

I have often been tempted to leave the matter alone, fearful lest the distorted conceptions of my hearers would make the truth that I sought to proclaim ridiculous in their eyes. But better counsels have prevailed, and, with all the earnestness of which I am capable, I am continually beseeching my audience to flee from the wrath to come, trusting the Holy Ghost to enlighten the understanding and reach the heart and conscience through the fearful words which He has indicted through the Apostle of love on the isle of Patmos.

I pass on to the other two objects which may be presented as a means of moving men.

Deep down in the human heart there is an instinctive craving for the perpetuity of life. The Lord Jesus was ever offering salvation on these terms and seeking to reach men through this avenue. All men, of course, will not be thus reached, but in our audiences and among our inquirers we shall meet with not a few who will respond just to that appeal.

The witness of the young priest that I have quoted in another connection might well be cited here also as a proof of this instinctive craving for Eternal Life within the souls of men. And yet in heathen lands souls so thoughtful as this young Buddhist priest are not often met with; and we shall find that an appeal to the instinct which desires eternal life will not often reach the mark.

Generally speaking, fear of death is a much more effective and a more usual means of awakening men. God has set it as a signpost on the road that leads to judgment. "It is appointed for men to die once, but after this the judgment" (Heb. 9:27). Though men may not know it, the sting of death's terror lies here. We can use the fact of death as a means of appeal. Once again, I will call the witness to tell how deeply and terribly real is the fear of death in a heathen soul. It is more than instructive to hear firsthand the thoughts and feelings that filled the heart of a heathen as he faced the King of Terrors unarmed and unprepared.

The following is the testimony of one who afterwards became an eminent saint, called not infrequently the

John Fletcher of Japan. He certainly breathed the spirit of that Apostle of love more than any man I have met East or West. This is how he writes:

> I was born in a Buddhist family. My mother was a very devoted believer, and she was very strict in bringing up her children in the Buddhist faith. I was never allowed to take my breakfast before I had gone to the family shrine to burn incense, bow before the idols, and repeat a short form of prayer. In the evening we gathered once more before the shrine ... When I was eighteen years old, I had a very bad fever and thought that I was dying. One day the doctor told my mother, and she told me ... I told her a few things that I wished done after my death, and I was reconciled to my fate and kept very quiet. But when I came face to face with death I was not satisfied with Buddha. There was no reality. Up till then I thought I was all right in Buddha and his salvation. But, alas! I had not peace ...
>
> Notwithstanding all that they preached about the future glory, as they called it, I had no desire to go; I was not ready; and there I found my need. I was not satisfied. I longed for something real, something that would satisfy my soul. I had no victory over death. But I knew no better at the time, so I simply kept quiet.

# THE SENSE OF NEED

> This is the condition of the heathen today: they are sitting in the dark and in the shadow of death. They are passing away without God. I shall never forget those days of waiting for death. It is awful thus to have to meet death face to face. I am so thankful that God in His mercy spared my life that I might be found of Him and be eternally saved!

Oh, that this testimony may stir our hearts to understanding something of the misery that lies concealed in the bosom of those who have never heard and stimulate us to present the blessed message of eternal life to those who sit in darkness and in the shadow of death!

I have endeavored to show the misery in a heathen soul as he faces death. In seeking to awaken souls, however, we shall take the greater pains to present to them the blessedness of a Christian deathbed. The horror of great darkness that besets the passing of an idolater is made all the more fearful by the light that shines upon the exodus of the Christian.

I was once called in to see a girl of some fifteen summers dying of consumption. I shall never forget the sight. She had been saved only about a year. She was emaciated beyond recognition, racked with intense suffering by her cruel malady. After an awful spasm of coughing, she turned to me with a radiant smile and said, "Oh, the joy! Oh, the joy! It's almost more than I can bear!"

I asked, "What joy?"

She replied, "The Lord Jesus! The Lord Jesus!" and then, in spite of her pain, tried to sing, "He's the One, the only One, the blessed, blessed Jesus, He's the One." After a line and a half, she broke out again into a shattering cough.

The doctor came in—a heathen—and looking at me said, "She's light-headed, I think."

I replied, "Nay, nay; she's light-hearted."

The heathen neighbors came in to see the passing of a little saint as she went into the presence of the King.

Yes, a victorious Christian deathbed is a glorious place to study Christian apologetics and awaken a slumbering sinner, if so be that he may hunger after that eternal salvation which alone will make him a living saint.

God shall bless us and give us souls for our hire and stars for our crown. So shall "the poor . . . the brokenhearted . . . the captives . . . the blind . . . and those who are oppressed" be blessed, bound up, healed, and saved of the Lord (Luke 4:18).

CHAPTER 8
# The Sense of Sin

> Being filled with all unrighteousness, sexual immorality, wickedness, covetousness, maliciousness; fall of envy, murder, strife, deceit, evil-mindedness; they are whisperers, backbiters, haters of God, violent, proud, boasters, inventors of evil things, disobedient to parents, undiscerning, untrustworthy, unloving, unforgiving, unmerciful . . . (Rom. 1:29-31)

In reading that remarkable book, *Lectures on Revival,* by Charles Finney, one cannot but be impressed with the fact how little he emphasizes the presentation of the winsomeness of the Gospel. He refers to it, of course, and all its blessings; but the main and mighty trend of all his remarks is the sin of rebelling, resisting, and rejecting God's offer of mercy.

This is proper in so-called Christian lands, where men and women have been made familiar with God's grace and blessing, and it is sin against Him that we need to emphasize. In heathen lands, however, the case is obviously far otherwise. Before there can be the sin of rejection, there must be a knowledge of what has been offered; before men can be convicted of sin in the deeper sense of the term, there must be a presentation of the Gospel blessing and an appeal to their sense of need rather than of sin; and yet I hasten to add that there can be no true and lasting experience of salvation without conviction of sin. Although generally speaking it is rather a sense of need in some form or other that in the first instance turns men heavenward, yet before long there must come conviction of sin not merely as it affects ourselves and others, but sin against a holy and righteous God.

The task is incomparably more difficult than that of awakening to a mere sense of need, for the simple reason that men are absolutely in the dark as to the existence, nature, righteousness, and the claims of the One against whom they have transgressed. Hence the word "sin" has no content or meaning in the Christian sense of that term.

In our attempt to produce conviction of sin, it is, of course, imperative that we speak in definite terms of moral corruption, profligacy, vice, and evil in all its forms. We must particularize and deal faithfully with these things, and yet that must never be our main objective. Sin in

# THE SENSE OF SIN 113

the proper and more fearful understanding of the word consists of man's violated relationship to God. As I have said elsewhere, we are commissioned to preach not repentance, but repentance toward Him. The essence of sin is man's rebellion against, alienation from, and hatred of God. "This is *the sin* of the world." All else are fruits from that evil tree. Our business, then, in the hands of the Holy Ghost, is to convict men of sin—"*the sin* of the world."

I would advance two very simple propositions. First, that there can be no true conviction of sin in its deepest sense without an understanding of God. The presentation, therefore, to a heathen of truth concerning His character and claims is so utterly fundamental that there can be no subject more important. Second, the main objective in our presentation of such truth should be to produce conviction of sin.

In the first chapter of the Epistle to the Romans, where St. Paul draws the veil aside from the unregenerate heart, he presents us with four very terrible pictures: a darkened mind; vile, unspeakable lust; unnatural passions; and every form of evil in action. But the Apostle takes great pains to tell us that these are only effects and not causes. The causes, he points out, are 1) "Although they knew God, they did not glorify Him as God, nor were thankful" (Rom. 1:21); 2) "They . . . changed the glory of the incorruptible God into an image made like corruptible man" (Rom. 1:23); 3) They "exchanged the truth of God for the lie . . . " (Rom. 1:25); 4) "They did not like to retain God in their knowledge" (Rom. 1:28). Conviction of sin, therefore, will be an unveiling of the causes of things rather than an exposure of the results, however shameful they may be.

In the story of the Prodigal Son, we find just the same thing. There is no recitation of all the sins and iniquities which he committed in the far country. They are dismissed in a single sentence. Only the cause is portrayed; only the outstanding sin is depicted—the sin against his father. He despised his love, scorned his authority, disregarded his tears, dishonored his name, flouted his patience, and wasted his goods. This was his sin, and, when he returned home broken with shame, he cried out, "Father, I have sinned against . . . you," as well as broken the laws of heaven (Luke 15:18).

The one word used in Scripture to denote sin is *unbelief*. It is a wide and comprehensive synonym. It means the rejection of God—His love, His claims, and His truth. It utterly denies that He lives and loves and cares and seeks and saves, blesses and protects, and would fain fill us with joy and lead us to eternal blessedness. It is a total rejection of it all. From this springs evil in all its forms; and it is of this that in the hands of the Holy Ghost we are commissioned to convict men and women.

Making inquiries of converts after they have been Christian for some years as to their first experience of conviction of sin, I have observed even in cases where a sense of sin as well as of need has influenced them to seek salvation, they have been unable to analyze their thoughts or say in what their sense of need consisted.

Certainly it was not sin against God; nor could they say it was a sense of sin against themselves or others. They seemed merely to realize that they had done things which instinctively they knew to be evil. The laws of God were written in their heart; and though the knowledge of the Lawgiver had been almost entirely effaced, yet there remained some traces of the Decalogue (however much they may have been blurred and scribbled over by superstition) as a standing witness against the violation of their conscience.

We need not be discouraged if in the early hearings of the Gospel a seeker has very little spiritual conception of sin; we may well be content if he only realizes that he has broken the law of God, as written in his heart. The cry, "Father, I have sinned against ... you," "Against You, You only, have I sinned," will be a later and deeper experience (Luke 15:18, Psalm 51:4). The sense of God's broken law will give way to the consciousness of his broken heart as he learns at the feet of the Savior and there understands the meaning of the Cross. Martin Luther once said, "I never knew repentance until I learned it from the wounds of Jesus." The sense of sinner-hood in the great majority of cases comes later.

How, then, shall we present the subject in such fashion as to create a real and genuine conviction of sin? I have found it helpful and effective to discover to one entirely uninstructed four simple aspects of the matter: Sin 1) as it affects ourselves, 2) as it affects others, 3) as a transgression of God's law, 4) as it grieves the heart of God.

## Sin as It Affects Ourselves

But he who sins against me wrongs his own soul. (Prov. 8:36)

Generally speaking, man's first understanding of sin is through its effect upon himself. Many times have I seen men and women brought to a place of the deepest conviction through such a word as "the wages of sin is death" (Rom. 6:23). Entirely ignorant of God and hence of sin against Him or His laws, they have been brought under deep conviction through the Holy Ghost as He has applied to their hearts this incisive message. It seems to sum up and concentrate in one brief, pregnant expression the reflection of many years' experience. Men are first made conscious of the evil consequences of sin rather than of sin itself.

Some years ago, a poor fellow who had come to the city where I am laboring had fallen into wicked and profligate ways, wasting all his substance in riotous living, till, without a friend in the world to whom he could turn for help, he could only think of murder and suicide as the way out of his difficulty. He therefore decided to kill his wife and three children, and then put an end to himself. He was dissuaded from his first intention by seeing his little boy smile in his sleep as he was about to plunge a dagger into his throat.

Forsaking his first intent, he sold all that remained to him of his scanty possessions, and, purchasing tickets for his wife and children, sent them home to her parents. He then started out to commit suicide. Passing by our tent, he entered in and dropped into a seat at the entrance. The first words that greeted his ear were, "The wages of sin is death." Dropping his head into his hands, he sat through the sermon but heard not a word. The arrow from the armory of God had pierced his heart. Through this shaft from Jehovah, the Holy Ghost convicted him of sin and kept him from his purpose. He was, however, entirely ignorant of the very first elements of Christianity.

The preacher, seeing him in distress, approached him, hoping that his discourse had given him some further light, and was not a little discouraged to find that nothing had entered either his head or his heart beside the words of Scripture. With infinite patience and sympathy, he heard his story, unfolded the truth, and led him to the Savior. For several weeks, he delighted every night to speak in the crowded tent of the salvation which he had found from sin and death and hell. He had not as yet any deep sense of sin against God or His laws; he only knew and felt that sin had brought him to the edge of the precipice; and this was enough to turn him to God and to the Savior as soon as he learnt of Him.

In seeking, then, to convict of sin, we need to emphasize its terrible effects. "But he who sins against me wrongs his own soul" (Prov. 8:36). I have found that in the case of an uninstructed heathen such a presentation is generally the first and most effective means of reaching his heart.

Here, however, I hasten to add an important consideration. When a seeker has traveled thus far, we need to show him that sin such as this not only pays its wages in the currency of death, but also causes an eternal separation from God. Sin is a separating thing. We should be very careful not to lose our opportunity of declaring the deeper view of sin to one who is thus convicted. We must at once take advantage of this elementary conception as a steppingstone to a higher and more thorough conviction. It is very easy to fail here and to leave the penitent only half-enlightened. We are in a position to make use of his trouble to show him the deeper and more spiritual aspect of sin against a Holy God, separating Him from us, and needing an atoning sacrifice.

## Sin as It Affects Others

Woe to him who increases what is not his . . . Woe to him who builds a town with bloodshed, who establishes a city by iniquity! . . . Woe to him who gives drink to his neighbor . . . even to make him drunk." (Hab. 2:6, 12, 15)

Without appealing to the supposed altruism in the heart of the sinner, we should seek to convict of sin by another method. We should show its evil effects upon others. Many a man has become a seeker of salvation because of the misery that his sinful life is causing his wife and children. The Scripture abounds in descriptions of sin as it affects others. In fact, all the main manifestations of sin are thus. By its fruits the evil tree can be known. We need, therefore, in seeking to convict of sin, to express in

# THE SENSE OF SIN

incisive language the devastating cruelties caused by the wickedness of men.

Some years ago, a man came to our mission hall in great distress, anxious to know if our religion could do anything for him. On inquiry we found him to be the victim of an ungovernable temper. On the previous day, in a fit of rage, he nearly murdered his wife, and would have succeeded if his neighbors had not come to the rescue. When his rage had cooled, he discovered how near he had been to disaster, and in not a little trepidation he started out to find the Salvation Army as the only agency likely to help him. He came to us instead, supposing, as I imagine, that we were an amateur branch of that institution. Thank God, the worker in charge was able to point him at once to a Savior, present, able, and willing to save him to the uttermost, even though heretofore he had known nothing whatever of Christianity. That was many years ago; and today he and his wife are still pressing on along the road to Zion. How true it is that sin introduces us to the Savior.

Here again we have a steppingstone to higher truth. When a man has been thus convicted of sin's disastrous effect upon others, it is not difficult to discover to him its more awful and terrible meaning. We need to be on the watch here, lest we lose our opportunity and allow the penitent to remain half-enlightened. So good an opportunity may not occur again, and we need to make use of the position that we have thus gained.

## Sin as a Transgression of the Law

Father, I have sinned against heaven ... (Luke 15:18)

We have already seen that a presentation of both the two preceding aspects of sin is only a steppingstone to something higher and more thorough. Sin as the Word of God declares it is a transgression of His law as written upon the heart and conscience of mankind. We must never rest satisfied until such is secured.

Although we need not be disappointed if we do not at once see it, yet I have been frequently astonished to see how swiftly the Holy Ghost can convict the most ignorant and uninstructed heathen of breaking the laws of God written upon even his darkened heart. I have seen cases where, apart from perceiving the evil results in himself and others, with very little sense of transgressing the laws of God, a man has had an extraordinary feeling of moral iniquity, though he might be unable to express in words its true import. Of course it is very easy to enlighten such a one and show him the true meaning of sin against God and His laws as the Scriptures unfold it.

Last year I was speaking at a small convention in a country town where a hundred and fifty Christians gathered for a week. In the audience there was the brother of one of the local Christians, a very ignorant peasant. He could neither read nor write. He had certainly heard little or nothing of Christianity before; hence it seemed very unlikely that he would derive any profit from the addresses, which were dealing with the baptism of the

# THE SENSE OF SIN

Holy Ghost, and the "rest [that remained] for the people of God" (Heb. 4:9). On the second day, however, after I had finished speaking and thrown the meeting open for prayer, in great distress and with very visible emotion, he was the first to respond. His prayer was somewhat as follows: "O God, I don't know anything about You; I can't read or write; I have never prayed in my life before; but please hear and answer my cry. I have committed such awful sins that I could never confess them here in public; but please have mercy upon me. Amen."

On the following day, after I had finished my address on the Second Rest, he struggled to where I was standing and appeared to be in the greatest agony of mind. He cried aloud, writhing on the ground like one possessed. Great beads of perspiration stood out on his forehead. His distress was fearful to witness. It took three men to hold him down and quiet him. I could but think of the judgment day when sinners shall stand before their righteous Judge.

He was taken to the vestry of the church, and in about half an hour God spoke peace to his soul as he rested on the atoning blood of the Redeemer. He subsequently returned home, a new creature in Christ Jesus. His old father was so amazed at the change in him that he at once expressed a desire that his son's God should be his God, and all the village were obliged to confess that the Christian's God had done great things for him.

I was amazed at the rapidity of the work of the Holy Ghost. The man seemed to have a fearful conviction of sin as the transgression of God's law written on his heart. Such instances, I know, are rare, but gloriously possible in answer to prayer when the Spirit is poured out from on high.

In any case, this should be our objective. Sooner or later, there must be an understanding of sin as a transgression of the law before a deep and satisfactory experience is assured.

## Sin Against the Father's Love

Father, I have sinned . . . before you. (Luke 15:18)

We pass now to the deepest and most searching conception of sin. We discover it to be not merely the breaking of laws, but of the heart of God. The story of the Prodigal illustrates this with exquisite simplicity. It starts with the fact of the Father. Take him out of the frame, and the picture collapses. There is no story left to tell! As I have often asked a heathen audience, if the boy had no father to return to, where would the story be? How could the boy have repented if he had no one toward whom to repent? The very essence of the story is the Father and His love. To demand a proof of the Father's existence is something akin to sacrilege. The fact of the son proves the fact of the father; and if common sense demands that such be so, how much more the heart? Yet true as all this is, truer still to life are men strangely delighted if they discover the vaporings of some clever fool who has proved to his own satisfaction either that there is no God at all, or that

He is so far removed from His own creation as to be a negligible quantity.

"Although they knew God, they did not glorify Him as God" (Rom. 1:21). The boy, knowing his father, honored him not as such; he wanted only to get his goods and then be gone. Men desire not God. And yet, as I tell my audience repeatedly, if the beautiful conception of a heavenly Father is not true, it ought to be. It is too beautiful not to be true. If we cannot believe it, we ought at any rate to want to believe it.

But alas! how different it all is in fact! Like the Prodigal in the story, so men in actual life do not want to believe any such thing because, like him, they love only the goods. Men are not thankful. *Greedy but not grateful* is written large over heathenism. Here is its hallmark: "The people sat down to eat and drink and rose up to play" (Ex. 32:6). This too is the hallmark of the Prodigal. All these things are so true to life that they carry conviction on their very presentation. Heathenism corroborates the pathos. The gods are mere pieces of convenience. They are believed in for what can be got out of them. Their worshippers care only for the goods; the gods can take care of themselves.

The facts of heathen religion are so like the sin of the son in the story that what otherwise might be regarded as a mere ideal now carries truth and reality on its very face. If the story is true in this and other sinister particulars, surely it must be true in its most beautiful one, namely, the existence of a loving Father in heaven.

Despising love is perhaps the cruelest thing on earth; it is the one unpardonable thing—worse than weakness, worse than lust, worse than deceit and all manner of evil. Open-handed sin against love scorns its tears and mocks at its heartache. It is brutal beyond all reckoning. Love rejected is the acme of evil; and this was the Prodigal's crime, this is the sin of humanity.

I have found it helpful to enlarge upon the nature of the love of God as given us, for instance, in such passages as Titus 3 and Ephesians 2, where the four words *kindness, love, mercy,* and *grace s*peak to us of its four wonderful aspects. 1) Forbearing love (Rom. 2:4): love that hesitates to punish, waits to be gracious, hopes against hope, lingers and dallies with the sword of justice. 2) Sacrificial love (John 3:16): the love which gives its best and brightest for the salvation of the worst and most uncomely. 3) Practical love (Titus 3:5): the love that provides a mighty regenerating power and gives the Holy Ghost to sanctify and renew. 4) Righteous love (Titus 3:7): the love which, rather than be false to justice, will suffer and bleed and die, and so make all its promises forever secure and forever irrevocable as the decrees of an Almighty God.

I like to think that the Prodigal, as he came home confessing his sin against heaven and against his father's heart, bethought him of the prophet's words: "Hear, O heavens, and give ear, O earth! For the Lord has spoken: 'I have nourished and brought up children, and they have rebelled against Me; the ox knows its owner and the donkey its master's crib; but Israel does not know, My people do not consider'" (Isa. 1:2–3). And yet again:"'Be astonished, O heavens, at this, and be horribly afraid; be very desolate,' says the Lord. 'For My people have committed two evils: they have forsaken Me, the fountain of living waters, and hewn themselves cisterns—broken cisterns that can hold no water'" (Jer. 2:12–13).

This more perfect and more spiritual conception of sin is rarely found in cases where there has been very little instruction of Bible truth; and yet I have found some notable instances. Here is one. Some years ago, I went to open a new town in a country district. The Gospel had never been preached there before. I took ten days' meetings, and on the first evening I spoke on the Prodigal Son.

On the following morning, a young girl of about nineteen came with her aunt to see me. Finding here an awakened and earnest seeker, I devoted a couple of hours to a study of the Word, and when, after a good deal of instruction, I turned to John 3:16, unfolding its blessed truth, she burst into tears. I think I have never seen either before or since an uninstructed heathen so deeply affected at so early a stage in their inquiry. In the sweetest simplicity and gratitude, she accepted the Gift of God through our Lord Jesus Christ and returned home resting on the promises of God.

The Lord at once began to use her. At the close of the mission, at about five o'clock in the morning, her old father came to my lodgings. I supposed that it was to bid me farewell, as I was leaving early that day. He soon undeceived me, however, by saying that he had come to get the joy his daughter had got. She told me subsequently that the old man had hardly slept at all that night, but kept inquiring "if it was not time to go and get the joy." Thank God, he got it that morning, and after living some years in happy service for his Lord and Master, he had a joyful entrance into the heavenly kingdom. He was the first of many souls won to the Savior by that dear girl. She still delights to tell of His abounding love and lead sinners to the Good Shepherd.

And so I bring this chapter to a close. To expect a heathen who hitherto has known nothing of these things to understand, to believe, and to feel the sense of sin such as I have described after one or two hearings of Christianity may appear unreasonable and unlikely enough; but I have found that by presenting the truth through such a story as the Prodigal Son, it does not take long for a heart prepared of the Holy Ghost to be truly convicted of sin against the living God.

## CHAPTER 9
# The Minimum of Truth

But the righteousness of faith speaks in this way, "Do not say in your heart, 'Who will ascend into heaven?'" (that is, to bring Christ down from above) or, "'Who will descend into the abyss?'" (that is, to bring Christ up from the dead). But what does it say? "The word is near you, even in your mouth and in your heart" (that is, the word of faith which we preach). (Rom. 10:6-8)

No one who has not made an attempt can fully realize the difficulty of the task to be undertaken by a preacher of the Gospel in heathen lands, if at least he does so with any expectation of seeing immediate results to his ministry. Consider for a moment the material he has at his disposal, or rather the lack of it. No allusion can be made to any of the facts of the Gospel or stories of the Old and New Testaments. The use of such words as *atonement, redemption, reconciliation, regeneration, Holy Spirit,* and indeed all the great words of Scripture are almost unintelligible. Words even for *sin* and *God* and *salvation* are often, if not always, unmeaning, at least in a Christian sense of the term. The hearer has no previous knowledge of any of the facts of the Christian religion through which the preacher can appeal, so any reference to the well-known Bible stories is ruled out of court. The mention of Abel, Noah, Abraham, Daniel, all the Old Testament worthies, or indeed of Christ Himself, conveys practically nothing to the mind. The understanding on all these things is a blank.

The purpose of the present chapter is an attempt to show the minimum of truth that needs to be presented before we can lead a seeking soul into the experience of salvation. I may say in passing that there is no subject that needs more reflection, study, prayer, and painstaking inquiry than this. I personally have spent very many long hours in studying how thus to present the minimum of truth in such a way as effectively to reach the hearts of men who know nothing whatever of the facts or truths of Christianity, and I make bold to say that no one will succeed unless he does the same.

I shall assume in this chapter that the one with whom we are dealing has been in a measure awakened to a sense of need, at any rate, if not of sin; or in other words that the inquirer is a genuine seeker. Knowing nothing whatever of Christianity, he has been aroused through trouble, sorrow, sickness, care, or the evil results of his sin, or maybe through some sermon that he has heard or book that he has read. He comes to us with a vague idea that by believing Christianity he can obtain peace of heart, deliverance from sin, and salvation in the life to come, though he may never express his need in these actual terms. How are we to proceed with such? What is the minimum of truth that he needs to know before we can urge him to believe and be saved?

## 1. To Present in the Words of Scripture That Aspect of Salvation Which Exactly Answers to the Express Need of the Seeker

If you knew the gift of God, and who it is who says to you, "Give Me a drink," you would have asked Him, and He would have given you living water. (John 4:10)

After ascertaining the line along which the seeker has been awakened, our first task is to present in Scriptural words that aspect of salvation which is answerable to his express need. We must focus the need for him; make it clear and definite; explain, unfold, and illustrate it in simple terminology; and finally fasten and clinch it with the Word of God. In other words, we must state the truth of the nature of salvation.

At the same time, we should take great care to follow up on the lines along which the inquirer has been awakened. If, for example, he is burdened about a judgment to come, it is no use presenting the truth of salvation in terms of present happiness or victory over sin, though of course we must refer to these things. If the penitent (a young man, perhaps) is deeply concerned about deliverance from the chains of lust, we must not practically ignore his difficulty by seeking further to awaken him on the lines of eternal life after death. Let our presentation of the truth be simple, single, and definite. Let it further be expressed in such a way that the penitent sees clearly the possibility of immediately receiving salvation as a gift.

The invariable tendency in the mission field of almost every seeker is to think that through a gradual understanding he will gradually drift into a gradual experience of a very gradual salvation. Such notions should, of course, be checked at the very outset. Salvation is a gift. In unfolding the nature of salvation, whether as promised rest of heart, the light of assurance, liberty from bondage, or eternal life, let us reiterate again and again with increasing emphasis that it is a gift—is something definite, something to be received, something to be had in a moment, and had now.

In presenting this truth thus, it is well to make the seeker read it as expressed in words of Scripture, and if possible memorize the particular passage, thus fastening it as a nail in a sure place. If all else is forgotten, that at any rate will abide.

Not long since, a young woman came in to the inquiry room who, though never having heard a word of the Gospel before, was awakened by the sermon she had heard to her sense of need. Discovering that it was upon the line of restless dissatisfaction, I at once opened my Bible and bade her read Matthew 11:28. This she did three or four times till she had memorized it. I fastened the word upon her heart, after carefully explaining its meaning. I then declared to her that this salvation was the gift of God to be asked for and received here and now.

## 2. A Clear and Simple Instruction of God as Father and Answerer of Prayer

If you then, being evil, know how to give good gifts to your children, how much more will your Father who is in heaven give good things to those who ask Him! (Matt. 7:11)

We pass naturally from the gift to the Giver. Here is the second aspect of truth that it is necessary to present to the inquirer: His existence, power, and, above all, His willingness to hear and answer prayer.

In the above-mentioned case, I had already spoken of God, dealing with the question of God as Father and Giver in the sermon which had caused her to come forward as a seeker. I discovered, however, that her mind was so occupied with her own need and distress that the existence and power of a living God to hear her cry and give what she needed had hardly entered her consciousness.

Now, in seeking to present instruction as to God's existence, nature, and claims, etc., to one who has not known of such things, the greatest care must be taken to eliminate all truth not necessary for the immediate matter in hand. We need to beware of two extremes: 1) a sentimental and emotional conception on the one hand; 2) a mere intellectual or academic notion on the other.

In the present case, I pressed upon the inquirer the fact that if there be such a thing as a living, personal God, *He surely must answer prayer.* I asked her to put the matter to the test. Does God actually answer prayer? We should read and explain carefully such a passage as Matthew 7:11; direct the heart solely to the truth contained in this passage; insist that the inquirer shall practically test the matter. At all events, avoid seeking to explain about God. Let the instruction about Him have a practical bearing on the case in hand. Beware of a lot of academic explanations as to His creatorship, power, omniscience, and omnipotence. Keep the penitent to this one simple, single idea, that God will hear and answer and give what we ask Him for.

This point is so important that I record a very striking story which exactly illustrates my meaning far better than I can explain. One of the most beautiful Christians I know in Japan, a lady suffering, I fear, from a most malignant malady, and yet evincing the sweetest confidence in God, at our hall a few Sundays ago asked if she might tell the people of her Savior and how she was found of Him. Though her voice was hardly strong enough to fill the hall, she held the audience, mostly men, for nearly forty-five minutes. I briefly relate her testimony:

> I was born and brought up in a little country town, with no opportunity of ever hearing of

God and His salvation. When about twenty years of age, I was engaged to be married, and all my friends were congratulating me. Their congratulations, alas! did not mean very much to me. I had such a view of the hollowness of life and was weighed down in consequence with such awful depression that I knew not whither to turn. I used to go up into the graveyard on the hillside where all my forebears were buried, and, looking over the little town, reflect that in a few short years all those who were now working and toiling to eat and drink and sleep would be lying by the side of their fathers. And then what—and whither? No one knew, and there was no one to tell me. What a strange mockery life appeared!

Again and again I meditated suicide. A friend, knowing of my melancholy, gave me a small copy of the New Testament. I opened it but could make nothing of it, and as there was no one to teach me I left it alone. So my misery went on, and I again decided to take my life.

While in this state of mind, I remembered reading a story of a Chinese soldier taken prisoner in the China-Japan War. He was brought to a military prison at Hiroshima, where a missionary got permission to visit him amongst others. He was entirely indifferent to such matters; but a little later, committing a serious offense, he was court-marshaled and condemned to death.

In his distress, he thought of the missionary and the books that he had brought. He had, however, no means of instruction, but he thought to himself, if the God of Whom he had just heard was a real, living God, surely He would answer prayer. He determined to put the matter to the test. Kneeling in his cell, he cried, "O God, if You are a real, living God, please hear and answer my petition, and send along the man who came to this prison, that he may teach me about You and the way of peace. If You answer my prayer, I will believe in You. Amen."

That night, the missionary in question was deeply impressed in his mind that he ought to visit the prison. On the following day, he proceeded thither. The man was overjoyed and at once led to the Savior. The change in his whole character was so sudden and marked that the military authorities, at first deferring the execution of the sentence, eventually reprieved him altogether, and at the close of the war he returned to China, there to preach the Gospel to his fellow countrymen.

I recalled to mind this story, and I said to myself, "Well, if that is true, I can do the same. I too will put God to the test." And so I prayed, "O God, if You are a real, living God, will You

> send someone to me in my misery, and show me the way of peace? If You answer my prayer, I will believe in You and try to serve You."
>
> An evangelist—Mizote San by name, living at Okayama, some considerable distance away—was that night similarly burdened in heart, and he said to his wife on the following day, "I feel I must go to K and see Miss —— ." He had once casually made my acquaintance.
>
> He appeared, to my unspeakable joy and amazement. It did not take him long to lead me to the Savior, and for now more than fifteen years I have loved and tried to serve Him.

Here is a very real secret in dealing with awakened souls, and a very blessed one. The seeker will thereby learn more of God in five minutes than in five months of theological study. So it was with the young woman in question.

Having proceeded thus far and carried her with me, being assured that she had grasped these two very simple ideas—God and His Gift—I then advanced a third step.

## 3. Intelligent Instruction on the Subject of Sin

Now we know that God does not hear sinners; but if anyone is a worshiper of God and does His will, He hears him. (John 9:31)

There is a blessed Gift to be had! There is a blessed God to give it to him that asks. Is there any reason why He cannot give, and any reason why we cannot receive? In nine cases out of ten, the seeker, when questioned, will see no reason at all, if only he asks sincerely with good intentions.

We need to inquire carefully of the penitent on this question. Get them to express their thought as clearly as possible on this point so that the subsequent instruction may have the more point and power. When they have thus expressed themselves, we must show them the separating power of sin. "Behold, the Lord's hand is not shortened, that it cannot save; nor His ear heavy, that it cannot hear. But your iniquities have separated you from your God; and your sins have hidden His face from you, so that He will not hear" (Isa. 59:1–2).

Here we shall need to spend some time. We must seek above all things to find out along which lines there is a sense of sin, if at all. Of course, each seeker will differ. We must not be discouraged if the sense of sin is not very spiritual. Use the Word of God freely and fearlessly. Do not be afraid that they will not understand it; but go back again and again to the original point—sin is a separating thing. God cannot hear until that is remedied. Insist upon this. Go over it repeatedly if need be. Much will depend upon the intelligence of the penitent, and also whether he is familiar with any degree of Christian truth, as to what illustration we can use or what passages of Scripture we can apply, and as to how we must deal with the seeker on this point.

Elsewhere I have pointed out that we use the word *sin* in a fourfold sense, denoting its guilt, its acts, its habits, and its in-being or nature. I have also endeavored to show that a seeker, though having no understanding of sin in the Christian sense, yet may realize it as either something damaging to himself or to others. This is, of course, a very inadequate sense of sin, but in dealing with a seeker on this subject we should be very careful to use even this as a steppingstone to a higher view. Take every advantage of his admissions to lift him higher. Never rest till he has a conception of sin against God, breaking both His laws and His heart. Sin is not merely a disease. It is an excluding, prohibiting, alienating thing. It excludes all communion with a Holy God, forever making the communication of His peace, purity, and power impossible till it has been recognized, confessed, self-judged, and dealt with by the great Sin-bearer.

To put it in other words, all consciousness of sin in act, habit, and in-being should be observed by the soul-winner and at once used to convict of guilt. The heathen know nothing of guilt by nature, even though they may be conscious of sin as damaging and evil in itself. Our task in dealing with a penitent who has been awakened to a sense of need and a belief that God can supply it, will be to show him the guilt of sin, though we shall need to deal with different men in different ways.

## 4. Instruction as to the Cross of Christ

And as it is appointed for men to die once, but after this the judgment, so Christ was offered once to bear the sins of many. (Heb. 9:27-28)

All we like sheep have gone astray; we have turned, every one to his own way; and the Lord has laid on Him the iniquity of us all. (Isa. 53:6)

The story is told of one under deep conviction of sin. Finding no relief, he called on an earnest Christian friend who, being very busy and having no time at his disposal to give to the anxious inquirer, hearing briefly of his trouble, replied, "Go home, open your Bible at Isaiah 53:6, go in at the first *all*, and come out at the second." With that, he bade him farewell and went on his way.

The heavy-laden sinner at first thought that his friend was jesting and went home somewhat ruffled. Turning, however, to the Book, he read: "All we like sheep have gone astray; we have turned, every one, to his own way."

"Well," said he, "that is true of me: I can certainly go in at that *all*."

"And the Lord has laid on Him the iniquity of us all."

"If that is true, then I can also go out at the second, and I am saved." Faith conquered, and he was free.

That is all easy enough for one brought up in a Christian land and familiar with Christian truth; but what about one who knows nothing of the life, death, and resurrection of Christ? Can he be instructed in one short hour sufficiently to exercise real, living faith in the Savior? To this I reply, "Yes, verily, if his heart has been prepared of the Holy Ghost."

We need to remember that it is not necessary to tell all the details of Christ's life and death and resurrection.

The fact of His atoning death and its intrinsic purpose and value are all that is necessary for our purpose. I say the historic fact of Christ's atoning death, because here in Japan, for example, the largest sect of Buddhism has practically invented a savior—Amida, a personage that never had any historic existence whatever. How blessed it is to tell them, not of a mythical redeemer, but of an historic Christ and His historic death and historic resurrection.

Faith in the Savior's blood is the mighty secret of our salvation. Till there is this, there is but little. Awakening, enlightening, repentance are only steps to this mighty, consummating step—faith in a crucified Savior. On this point above all other the enemy of souls seeks to deceive and to delude. The Devil cares not what a seeking penitent does if only he stops short of faith in the atoning work of the Son of God. One of the most pathetic sights is to see earnest souls floundering about in the quicksand of good resolutions, devoted endeavor, etc., ignorant of this Rock upon which He would fain plant their sinking feet.

In dealing with men on this most vital of all points, we shall need to present the truth by means of simple illustrations, differing, of course, according to their intelligence and viewpoint. To one we may speak of the blood as removing stains of condemnation; to others, we may present the Cross as a vicarious sacrifice; to another, Christ bearing our sins like the scapegoat of old; to another, the healing of the wounds and poison of sin through a vision of the brazen serpent; to another, we shall speak of redemption through blood; to yet another, of the price paid for our reception of God's Holy Spirit.

In all these cases, we shall need to observe carefully which of them is most easily understood and made most effective to different classes of people, and so use them accordingly.

I do most earnestly urge all my young missionary brethren to emphasize this vital point, to assume nothing, to take nothing for granted, not to suppose "He is in the company" when He is not, and never to rest until assured that the penitent is consciously resting on the atoning blood of the Redeemer.

From a long and varied experience, I am convinced that a simple and lucid presentation of these four facts—God and His Gift, sin and its remedy—are all that are required to enlighten unto salvation any soul whose heart has been prepared of the Holy Ghost in places of sin, sorrow, suffering, and woe.

In closing, there is one point that needs special emphasis. We should not be discouraged if in the case of those who have never heard before there seems almost no sense of sin; and if though apparently earnest and sincere in their seeking they apprehend no more than the first two glorious truths—God and His Gift. Above all, do not let us say to such, "Tomorrow." Grace and faith always say, "Today," and the Holy Ghost says, "Today," and, "Now is the day of salvation" (2 Cor. 6:2).

There is a way open even for such semi-prepared hearts. God has given to us the privilege and power of helping them into the Kingdom. Those wonderful words,

"If you forgive the sins of any, they are forgiven them; if you retain the sins of any, they are retained" (John 20:23), are for His ministers, if only we know how to use them in the confidence of faith.

Often as I have knelt beside a sinner seeking only "according to his light" deliverance from his sins, I have pleaded the blood of Christ and claimed for him the pardon of all his transgressions. He had only caught a glimpse of the gift and the Giver; he saw not yet his sin and Sin-bearer. He thought he needed but deliverance. I knew he needed, "Son, your sins are forgiven you" (Mark 2:5); and Christ, as of old, seeing the faith of the fisher of men, has blotted out all his transgressions and revealed the fact to him by a divine illumination of His Spirit not many days hence.

Following such lines as these, I succeeded in leading to the Savior the young woman with whom we started in our present chapter. Three days later, she came to tell me how God had filled her heart with peace, and though she hardly knew as yet the cause and secret of her joy, she could say, "One thing I know: that though I was blind, now I see" (John 9:25).

Such, then, I conceive to be the minimum of truth that we need to present to awakened souls.

CHAPTER 10
# The Minimum of Works

What must I do to be saved? (Acts 16:30)

If "What must I *know* to be saved?" was the contents of our last chapter, "What must I *do?*" will be the burden of this. We again assume that we are dealing with an awakened soul. Following, moreover, on the lines already laid down, and having given sufficient instruction on the four vital questions of God and His gift, sin and its remedy, we may further assume that the seeker turns to us with, "What, then, must I do to be saved? How can what you have told me be realized in my experience?"

In making reply, we need to observe four simple principles of action, for there are, in fact, four very plain duties to be performed on the part of the penitent ere he can obtain the full assurance of his personal salvation and acceptance with God. These we take in order.

## 1. Confession of Sin

If we confess our sins, He is faithful and just to forgive us our sins and to cleanse us from all unrighteousness. (1 John 1:9)

When the question was asked by the Philippian jailer, "What must I do to be saved?" St. Paul replied, "Believe on the Lord Jesus Christ" (Acts 16:31). It looks for the moment as though the confession of need and sin were unnecessary. This is really not so; for in dealing with the man more particularly, we read that "they spoke the word of the Lord to him" and took him down into the waters of baptism, an open and outward profession of his sinnerhood; and we may rest assured that in prayer there was the deepest confession both of his sin and his need.

From a long and wide experience, I have found that confession of sin on the part of the penitent is most important. Thereby we take Christ as our Sin-bearer. The transfer of our iniquities upon Him is thereby accepted by us. Subsequently by an act of faith we take Him as our savior.

We need to insist upon this! The seeker may have never prayed before. It matters not. However brief, however feeble the prayer and confession may be, he needs to pray. The cry, "God be merciful to me a sinner" (Luke 18:13), if it come from the heart, is enough. There is a mischievous tendency in the mission field, as at home, to substitute all sorts of things for this important duty. Men fancy they can be saved by understanding the truth, joining the Church, making resolutions, or giving up their sins.

There is a further tendency on the part of the worker to think that the seeker, not having learnt any form of prayer, cannot confess his sins at once. Let no such foolish considerations influence us in the least. Nay, rather let us seek to help, encourage, and guide the penitent into the performance of this duty from the very first.

As to the practical bearing of this important matter, let me illustrate. A young man of the student class once came to me expressing a desire to be a Christian. He told me that he had been attending church, studying Christianity for eight years, but still had one or two points to be cleared up ere he could decide to believe!

Taking out my watch, I told him that, as he had had eight years of instruction, I could tell him how to be saved in eight minutes. Somewhat surprised, he asked me how. I opened my Bible at 1 John 1:9 and bade him read, adding that if he would humble his heart, confessing his sin and need, God would certainly save him without delay.

This seemed to stimulate his memory, for he suddenly recollected that he had an important engagement, needing immediate attention. Promising to call again on the morrow, he hastened away; and I saw him no more! Much time, energy, and temper would thus be saved if we knew how to deal with captious Pharisees.

Another illustration with a happier sequel may not be out of place. In a previous chapter, I told the story of a drunken fisherman, now an earnest evangelist. His conversion was so striking an instance of the matter in hand, that I continue the narrative. Having been awakened, enlightened, and repentant, he had succeeded in breaking off most of his sinful acts and turned God-ward. But his evil habits held him in bondage. He was yet unsaved. The drink was entirely too much for him. He was still a drunkard, not infrequently attending the meetings the worse for liquor!

I had not yet met him, but calling one day at the outstation where he lived, I sent for him. He came sober! Questioning him, I found that he believed in all the fundamentals of the Christian faith, having been instructed by the worker in that place. He longed to be delivered, and yet was a puzzle to himself; he knew not why he was a slave, as he seemed willing enough to turn to the Lord, be baptized, and join the Church.

Finally, I asked him if he had ever confessed his transgressions, come to God as a poor lost sinner, and cried for mercy. To this he replied in the negative. Pride of heart, it seems, is possible even in a drunkard. I insisted that this must be done, and when he said that he had never prayed in his life, I suggested that it was about time he began. I held him to it. My fellow worker and I bowed in prayer, and, finally, with beads of perspiration standing out on his forehead, he burst forth in confession of his sin and need.

At once faith sprang up in his heart. In a moment, he was freed from his shackles and saved of the Lord. From that day, nearly twenty years ago, he has never tasted a drop of drink, and he has been rejoicing in God his Savior, winning souls for Him.

The matter is so important that I add a few words on its philosophy. The word runs, "If we confess our sins" (1 John 1:9), *not,* "If we ask for forgiveness." There is an immense moral difference between these two, whether we look at them in reference to the character of God, the sacrificial work of Christ, or the condition of the soul.

1) *The Character of God.* He has been perfectly satisfied as to all our sins by the Cross of Christ. He needs no further propitiation. We need not supplicate Him to be "faithful and just," for these qualities have been displayed, vindicated, and answered in the death of Christ. God does not need anything to draw His heart to the sinner.

2) *The Sacrifice of Christ.* Often in praying for forgiveness we thereby lose sight of the perfect ground of forgiveness, the Cross. Our prayer for pardon, however earnest, cannot form the basis of God's faithfulness and justice in the forgiveness of our sins. In the Lord's Prayer, we are told to ask for forgiveness, but in that case it is the forgiveness rather of sins of omission—debts, as they are called. Where sins of commission are concerned, there has to be a definite confession of the same in humility of heart. When this has been done, we can at once rest on the atoning blood of Christ.

3) *The Condition of the Soul.* Confession involves self-judgment. It is much easier to ask for pardon in a general way than to confess our sins in all their naked shame. If a child has done wrong, it is much less difficult to ask to be forgiven than openly and ingenuously to confess the wrong.

I came across an instance of this while on my recent furlough. I had been taking a series of meetings on Scriptural holiness. At the close, a lady came to me saying that one sentence I had spoken had set her soul at liberty from a bondage of some years' standing. On my making inquiry as to what it might be, she replied, "You said if God has been convicting you and revealing your inward sin and need, whatever you do, don't cry for deliverance! I was so astonished at this amazing statement that I looked up, wondering whatever you would say next, when you proceeded thus: The Word of God does not say, 'If we cry for deliverance, God is faithful and just to forgive us our sins and cleanse us from all unrighteousness,' but it does say, 'If we confess our sins.' I saw at once the difference and my mistake. I hastened home to my room, and getting down before God, told Him that, though I had long been crying for deliverance, it had never come. From that hour, I ceased my cry, and instead poured out my heart in honest confession of my sin. That very night, the Lord fulfilled His promise and set me free."

Let it be so with the sinner. Let us insist upon this fundamental duty before we urge the exercise of faith in the promise of God! As he inquires, "What must I do to be saved?" let us see to it that he makes a humble and hearty confession of sin to Almighty God, expressing in brokenness of heart and sincerity of purpose his need of saving grace. This is the first and all-important condition for receiving salvation.

## 2. Receive the Gift of God through Faith in the Promise

... exceedingly great and precious promises, that through these you may be partakers of the divine nature ... (2 Pet. 1:4)

Then those who gladly received his word were baptized. (Acts 2:41)

Receive with meekness the implanted word, which is able to save your souls. (James 1:21)

We have seen in our previous chapter that the objective of the soul-winner is to cause men to receive the gift of God, which is eternal life. The medium which God has appointed is His own Word.

I cannot emphasize too strongly the need of young missionaries observing this important factor in the salvation of souls. The Word of God not only enlightens and convicts—it is the means whereby life is conveyed to the spirit; it is the channel through which the living water flows; it is the seed from which there springs the living organism; it is the rope on which the drowning soul lays hold and clings till he is drawn safe to land. See to it that the seeking soul rests upon the promise of God, and that through faith in it he believes God Himself. We shall be tempted to try some other way, but beware of all substitutes.

It is well to exhort, warn, explain, pray, testify, and urge men to believe, but in the last analysis we must "implant the engrafted word," so that subsequently when faith is tested and all feeling, emotion, and enthusiasm have subsided, the soul may rest on the eternal Word of the Living God, which lives and abides forever.

In order to get the seeker to receive God's gift of eternal life in definite fashion here and now, we shall need, of course, to present a very definite promise. Mere vague persuasion, or the statement of the blessing, or even the presentation of "general truth," if I may use the phrase, is futile. We shall need to select a clear, appropriate, and definite promise and then get the penitent to read, re-read, repeat, and memorize it, so that when all else is forgotten, that shall abide, take root, and fructify unto eternal life.

Those of us who have had any real spiritual experience ourselves know well enough that as we walked through the valley of the shadow of spiritual darkness and desolation (yea, and of death itself to the world and all its vanities), it was the "rod and staff" of His Word that "comforted us" and brought us through into the land of life and glory. There is no substitute for this, and as the penitent asks, "What shall I do to be saved?" see to it that you reply, "Receive with meekness the engrafted Word which is able to save your soul."

In the parable of the sower and the seed, we read, "Then the devil comes and takes away the word out of their hearts, lest they should believe and be saved" (Luke 8:12). Surely the plain inference is that there can be no saving faith unless the Word of God is implanted within the soul. Take that away, and the enemy of souls knows well enough that deep impressions, good resolutions, yea, and the understanding of the principles of Christian truth, will avail nothing; they will be scattered as chaff before the wind, and the soul shall be as barren as sand in the wilderness. The only thing that lives and abides is the Word of God. Prayer is the cry of the drowning man for help. It is our business in response to throw him the rope. That rope is the promise of God. However strong a grip he may have, unless he has something to lay hold of, he will but grip the air and perish.

### 3. The Exercise of an Act of Faith in the Blood of Christ

If you can believe, all things are possible to him who believes. (Mark 9:23)

Faith as an act or definite exercise of the will, faith as a gift of assurance, and faith as a habit of the soul are three entirely distinct things. The gift of assurance, of which St. Peter speaks when he writes as having "obtained . . . precious faith," is bestowed of God (2 Pet. 1:1). The habit of faith is that gracious state of heart maintained by the Holy Ghost. But faith as an act or exercise is the work of the penitent himself, and it is of this, and this alone, that we are speaking here. Without it there is but little. It is this exercise of faith that makes it possible for God to bestow. Confession of sin and the implanting of the Word are both necessary, but unless they lead to such an exercise of faith the soul is not saved!

Such a faith as this presupposes several things: the *One* in whom the soul believes, the *medium* whereby he believes, the *reason* for which he believes, the *object* he is seeking to obtain, and the *groundwork* or foundation upon which he rests. The Person whom he believes is, of course, the living God; the medium, the written Word or promise; the reason, his own sin and need; the object for which he seeks, salvation; but the ground upon which he rests is the atoning sacrifice of the Savior. It is here that we need to direct his attention and insist that by an act of his will he rests and abides. It is to this the Spirit of God in His regenerating work alone responds. As Christian in the *Pilgrim's Progress* looked expectantly at the Cross, his burden rolled away, and the three shining ones appeared, clothing him in the garment of regeneration and giving him the assurance of his acceptance with God.

Do let us remember the fatal tendency of every child of Adam to substitute anything for faith in the Cross. I have often observed, in dealing with earnest Christians who are seeking for the fullness of the Holy Ghost, the same tendency in grounding their faith, or perhaps I should say, their endeavor upon a false foundation.

The illustration frequently used in devotional books is so misleading that I refer to it here. The fullness of God's gift is likened to an overflowing reservoir of water, the heart of the believer to an empty vessel, and between them is a pipe, adjusted to convey the water from the reservoir to the empty receptacle. If there be no inflow, an investigation reveals the presence of an object blocking the channel. Let that be removed, and automatically the vessel is filled.

Now this illustration, partially true and helpful in certain particulars, is egregiously misleading. The removal of hindrances represents repentance and consecration, but it is emphatically untrue that either repentance or consecration brings an automatic inflow of the Spirit of God into the heart. Alas! how many have tried, and tried in vain, to induce the Spirit of God thus to enter the sanctuary of their soul. He can, however, never enter so! He will respond only to one thing—faith in the blood of Jesus. Repentance and consecration there must be, but that which brings the Holy Ghost into the heart is an exercise of faith in the sacrifice of the Redeemer. The blood was shed to purchase that gift; and the faith that exalts and honors, trusts in and pleads that priceless thing, is alone acceptable unto God. To that alone will He respond and bestow His mighty gifts.

Not long since, when conducting a series of meetings for a missionary community, I took occasion to emphasize this point. One who was present, an earnest and devoted man, told me after the meeting had closed how this had come as a revelation to him. For many years, he had sought to enter the promised land by his repentance and consecrations. As he said, he had spent his time removing the hindrances, only to find there was no automatic inflow of the Spirit of God into his heart. During the meetings, one night he found himself awake and alone in the night watches; the Lord brought to his mind the story of the Israelites crossing the Jordan and reminded him that, though they had to sanctify themselves and put away all uncleanness before they could pass over, yet it was not that that brought them in. It was only the Ark of the Covenant borne on the shoulders of the believing priests that divided the waters. So did they go over dryshod. How he rejoiced in the way of faith after that, and there alone with God he hastened over into the promised land.

It is not otherwise with salvation, and we must above all things insist that the penitent, by an act of will, exercise faith in the atoning blood. That is the Rock upon which the feet, lifted from "the horrible pit" of despair and the "miry clay" of sin, must stand before their steps can be established or they can be saved from slipping back again into the quagmire of evil and the pit of shame (Psalm 40:2). In presenting this duty to the seeker, we need to make it plain that this exercise of faith is a single, definite act of will, to be performed once and for all, and, if real, should find expression in thanksgiving and praise.

As I have said, we can help him in this. We need to believe with him and for him, and thus help him into the Kingdom of God. We should present a promise containing exactly what he has to believe. Mere talk about the sacrifice of Calvary and Christ dying for our sins will not generally avail. There has to be an appropriation of Christ's salvation. The exercise of faith has to be definite, simple, and immediate. Insist upon this.

## 4. The Confession of Christ with the Mouth

With the heart one believes to righteousness, and with the mouth confession is made to salvation. (Rom. 10:10)

There is yet one other important duty to be observed in order to ensure the salvation of the soul. Before the witness of the Spirit is vouchsafed, God always demands a simple act of obedience to test the reality of faith. It is generally in the performance of such an act that the witness of the Spirit is bestowed.

The performance of this duty finds expression in many ways. First and foremost, as among the Jews or high-caste people of India, is baptism, which is regarded as the only sign or badge of true discipleship. And yet long before a convert is sufficiently prepared and instructed for baptism, it is most important that on the very day of his conversion he should at once confess Christ. The destruction of his idols, the observance of the Sunday, the refusal to accompany his old companions to places of pleasure and sin, all provide ample opportunity for confessing Christ.

Whatever form the expression of that testimony may take, we need to insist very strongly on its reality and thoroughness. "For whoever is ashamed of Me and My words in this adulterous and sinful generation, of him the Son of Man also will be ashamed when He comes in the glory of His Father" (Mark 8:38). The convert must burn his bridges behind him; he must put himself on record, and thereby save not only himself but maybe also those that hear him.

The Salvation Army were always past masters in this work. From the moment of conversion, the convert was instructed and urged to be a winner of others. The importance and value of testimony is threefold: 1) to strengthen the convert's faith, courage, and character; 2) to bring glory to Christ; 3) to convey salvation and blessing to others.

Let the philosophy of personal testimony be explained and made clear to the young convert from the beginning, and then let us insist that he obey God and openly confess his Master. By the confession of his sins, he takes Christ as his Sin-bearer, by the exercise of an act of faith he takes Him as his Savior, and by the confession of Him with his lips he takes Him as his Master and Lord. How many professed converts are unsatisfactory in their subsequent walk because they fail thus openly to declare the profession of their faith.

CHAPTER 11
# Salvation

... that they may receive forgiveness of sins and an inheritance among those who are sanctified by faith in Me. (Acts 26:18)

The supreme undertaking of the minister of Jesus Christ is to be the means in God's hands of conveying eternal life to a dead soul.

Investigating the great commission given to St. Paul, we have considered the task of awakening, enlightening, and converting the sinner dead in trespasses and sins. All this, however, is only preliminary to the main objective, i.e., only a preparing of the soul to receive the gift of God.

The salvation of the Lord Jesus Christ is salvation from sin. When we speak thus, we use the word in four distinct senses, as I have already pointed out—its guilt, its acts, its habits, and its nature or in-being. From all of these, the Lord Jesus has provided a full and perfect deliverance; we should never rest content until, first in ourselves and then in them that hear us, this salvation has been effectively realized.

To put the matter in yet other words, the salvation of the soul as secured for us by the Son of God, means first a *conscience* made void of offense toward God and men, and secondly a *heart* renewed through the Holy Ghost. It means justification and sanctification; it means forgiveness of sins and the new birth of the soul. These two blessed gifts of God, though coincident in experience, are entirely distinct in fact and meaning. The former deals with sins committed and their guilt; the latter with sin, its habit and its in-being.

## Salvation from the Guilt of Sin

. . . a conscience without offense toward God . . . (Acts 24:16)

Professor Charles Finney, in his lectures on revival, was always insisting, and rightly so, that it is the conscience with which the preacher has to deal. Here is one of his striking paragraphs:

> A minister should address the feelings enough to secure attention, and then *deal with the conscience* and probe to the quick. Appeals to the feelings alone will never convert sinners. If the

preacher deals too much in these, he may get up an excitement and have wave after wave of feeling flow over the congregation; and people may be carried away as with a flood and rest in false hopes. The only way to secure sound conversions is to deal with the conscience. If attention flags at any time, appeal to the feelings again and rouse it up, but do your work with conscience.

Now just as this is true in the *conviction* of the sinner, so it is true in dealing with his salvation. It is with the conscience we have to do. When awakened and alive with conviction, it is the conscience we must set at rest. The heart has to be changed, but before that can be, the wounded conscience must find balm and healing in the wounds of Jesus.

It is very easy to miss the way here! It is very easy to let the conscience be satisfied with works of repentance, restitution, reparation, and reformation. Now necessary as all these are in their place, to render the conscience void of offense toward men, they can never make it void of offense toward God.

A conscience void of offense toward God is not the mere non-consciousness of evil. This, of course, is necessary: "For if our heart condemns us, God is greater than our heart . . . " (1 John 3:20). But the absence of condemnation does not constitute a conscience void of offense toward God. To suppose that it does means a very egregious mistake. How many have rested in clearing their conscience of all sense of condemnation by a practical repentance toward their fellow men, yea, and a clearing that has cost them much in sacrifice and humiliation, and yet know nothing of the peace which passes all understanding, the blessed product of a conscience void of offense toward God? That can be secured only by the blood of Jesus. Forgiveness, and with it peace of conscience, can only come so. Our blessed task is to bring men there and introduce them to a Christ who bids us come *with* our sin.

> Come with thy sin,
> Come with thy sin,
> Jesus will save thee,
> Come with thy sin.

Now this is of all things the most difficult. Men will come to Christ with good resolutions, earnest endeavors, promises to lead a new life, but to come with their sin, i.e., in humble, straightforward confession, is what men hate above all things to do. And yet this is the only way. Christ came to save none but sinners; and as I often tell my inquirer, if you are not a sinner, there is no hope for you in time or eternity.

Or if we do succeed in getting men to come thus, there is the still greater difficulty in getting them to leave their sin with the Savior. They come and come again, taking their burden back with them every time. They fail to leave it once for all and forever at His feet, wondering withal that they have neither peace nor joy in believing. In other words, there is no harder task for the soul-winner to accomplish than to lead the sinner to a real believing confidence in the blood of Christ. An ignoring of that blood and putting in its place our own striving and willing, our endeavors and resolutions, our repentances and consecrations, can only be grieving to the Holy Ghost, who must ever refuse to bear witness to such, as long as there is no cordial acceptance of so sovereign a remedy provided by our gracious God. There may be an intellectual assent and understanding of the doctrine of redemption, but until the heart closes in with Christ, the gnawings of conscience are only numbed and will break out afresh in remorseless agony on that day when we have to give an account of the deeds done in the body, whether they be good or whether they be evil.

## Salvation from the Acts of Sin

. . . a conscience without offense toward . . . men. (Acts 24:16)

I have no doubt that some, reading these pages, may have been impressed that there has been so little said as to bringing forth "fruits worthy of repentance" (Matt. 3:8).

I have more than once insisted that the seeker should bring his sins to Christ, instead of seeking to break them off in his own strength. Here I would both correct and corroborate that statement a little more particularly. The greatest pains must be taken in distinguishing between sinful habits and sinful acts. The former will only be taken away by an operation of the Holy Ghost in the new birth. The latter must be dealt with by acts of repentance on the part of the sinner himself.

Let me take a supposed case. Here is a young man of dissolute habits, a slave to drink and lust and other forms of evil. He has become awakened, enlightened, convicted, and penitent, desirous above all things of being delivered from these habits that hold him in bondage. He has tried every means in his power to break his chains, only to fail again and again. A further inquiry into his life reveals that he is committing certain evil acts; we find dishonesty in business, association with evil companions, disobedience and ingratitude to his parents, unfaithfulness to his employers, etc.

These things are not habits. They are definite acts of unrighteousness which can and must be repented of and put away by the penitent himself. He must repent. There must be a conscience void of offense toward man. Such a conscience can be produced only through a practical repentance. It is vain for him to trust in the blood of Jesus, cry to God for mercy, or seek deliverance from the bondage of his evil passions as long as he refuses to obey God and turn away from these evil things.

Let him not say he has no power to do so. He has. Point out the distinction between these things and his evil habits. It is God's business to deal with the latter. It is his business to deal with the former and at once abandon his evil ways.

There is still a further and deeper difficulty with which the soul-winner is confronted and of which I must speak. Practical repentance does not merely consist in putting away all known sin out of the life; it may, and generally does, involve certain acts of restitution, reparation, and confession. And here we need much grace, wisdom, and discretion.

I have observed in not a few cases (my own among the number) that God in His gracious wisdom does not reveal to the penitent this important duty at the time of his conversion. Not till he has been established in grace and tasted the joy of salvation does the Spirit of God bring to his memory matters that have to be confessed, money that has to be restored, bitterness that has to be forgiven, reparation and restitutions that have to be made. Sometimes I know these fruits worthy of repentance are demanded at the hour of conversion, but in many cases not. The soul-winner, however, when he fails to lead a soul into lasting peace and can find no adequate reason, may well apply the searchlight here.

Out of my many instances I will call but a single witness. One, now in heaven, was seeking most earnestly peace of heart and conscience. Very swiftly to her honest heart did the Spirit of God reveal a sin committed years before in her childhood, demanding confession and forgiveness. Thank God she obeyed, and at once her conscience, now void of offense toward man, was able to rest in the finished work of Christ and so receive His full salvation.

The soul-winner, in dealing with such cases, will need much wisdom, grace, and tact. He will beware lest there be anything in his method that savors of that soul-destroying thing, the Roman Confessional. Again and again, as I have tried to help souls, I have told them not to tell *me* the sin, but only those whom it concerns, and then God. When, however, they have insisted on letting me hear their troubles, that I might advise them the better, I have in some cases suffered it. In others, when the sin has been of the vilest, I have refused to listen, lest my own mind and heart should be defiled. I have besought the penitent to let no ears but those of God listen to such confessions, marveling in my heart that the spotless One, the Lamb of God, can be unsullied by such unspeakable filthiness conceived, perpetrated, and uttered by the sinful sons of men.

Let us look well to our task. On the one hand, we have to beware of leading the soul to a supposed faith in the blood of Jesus without any practical repentance toward man; and on the other we need to take heed lest the seeking soul rest satisfied with his repentance and never rest upon the sacrifice of Christ. The forgiveness of sins—blessed gift! This is what we are called upon to cause men to receive.

Before closing this part of our subject, there is just one other point of importance that should be emphasized by the young missionary, namely, the clear distinction that needs to be observed in seeking to unfold the good news of the forgiveness of sins. In Scripture, this expression is used in two senses:

1. The initial experience denoting an act, once and for all and forever, consequent on our laying down our arms of rebellion: reconciliation with God. This wonderful gift need never be forfeited, and we may hope seldom is, but yet may be, as the parable in Matthew 18:23–35 and many other Scriptures plainly teach.
2. The subsequent forgiveness as a child of God, when and if he grieve Him by some act of sin and disobedience. The forgiveness of a rebel is one thing; the forgiveness of a child is quite another. Let us make and keep this distinction very clear, lest we and those we teach be brought into confusion and darkness.

## Salvation from the Presence and In-Being of Sin

O wretched man that I am! Who will deliver me from this body of death? I thank God through Jesus Christ our Lord! (Rom. 7:24–25)

It is a wonderful, wonderful thing for any soul to be brought out of the bondage of Egypt through God's justifying and regenerating grace. But alas! both we ourselves from our own experience and those with whom we deal soon discover that all the Egypt is not out of us when we are first converted to God.

Not one in a thousand has found it to be so! As workers together with God, our blessed duty is to lead those whom God has saved into all the *fullness* of salvation. The conscience is cleansed through a true repentance both toward God and man and a faith in the blood of Jesus. The heart has been changed, the will renewed, and we have been made new creatures in Christ Jesus. The guilt, the acts, the habits of sin have thus all been removed, but the in-being of sin remains. The *phronema sarkos* doth yet remain in the regenerate, as the Article of the English Church has it. It is deliverance from the presence of sin in the heart, the cleansing of the soul from "indwelling sin," "the evil heart of unbelief," "the carnal mind," "the body of sin," "the husband," "the superfluity of naughtiness," "all unrighteousness," that we need to present and offer to the hungry, seeking soul (Rom. 7).

In Romans 5 and 6, we read of a conscience cleansed and quickened, a will renewed, crucified, and risen with Christ, and a walk in the newness of life; but the seventh and eighth chapters tell of a deeper union than that of life, a union of marriage and fruitfulness, a union that can never take place till the old husband, i.e., sin in our members, that which is, "no longer I . . . but sin that dwells in me," has been done away by the Cross. The law which is holy (commanding the marriage), just (forbidding it as long as the husband lives), and good (showing the way of deliverance) will tolerate no divorce and resolutely forbid the banns to be published, until, like St. Paul, we have cried out, "O wretched man that I am! Who will deliver me from this body of death?" and have found in the wounds of Jesus a perfect healing, in His Cross a perfect destruction of the body of sin, and in His blood a perfect cleansing from its taint, as applied to our hearts by the Holy Ghost. Then can the marriage bells ring! Then we not only walk with Him in newness of life, but also serve Him in newness of spirit and bring forth fruit unto God!

This wonderful experience, like the new birth, is received by faith and is instantaneous in its reception. The Holy Ghost Himself (like His regenerating work in conversion) comes suddenly to the temple of the believing soul. There are many preparatory experiences, but the final bestowal is instantaneous. As Wesley says, a man may be a long time dying, but the actual article of death supervenes in a moment.

Now in seeking to help the convicted one into a full salvation, we must be careful of our diagnosis. We must be sure that the seeker is already a child of God and has passed from death unto life. Many a hungry soul is merely religious, knowing nothing of God's regenerating grace. It is useless for such to seek the "second blessing," if I may be pardoned for using so hackneyed a phrase. We shall only land them into darkness and confusion if we talk to them of these deeper things.

At a convention held for missionaries in Japan, dealing with this fuller experience, a lady attended the closing meeting. It was with the greatest difficulty that her friends could induce her to come even to that, so prejudiced was she against anything that savored of dissent or nonconformity. She came, however, under protest, and there God met with her. Her hungry heart was convicted of a deep need. She knew not what she wanted, but she knew she wanted something.

After three days of misery, she called to see me. I sought to diagnose her case. Perceiving her ignorance of the very fundamentals of God's saving grace, I asked her if she were willing to begin at the very beginning.

"I will begin anywhere if I can only get peace," she cried.

"But suppose you have to tell the authorities of your Mission that you have hitherto known nothing of a true conversion?" I said.

"I will tell anybody anything," was her answer, "if only God will bring rest to my troubled heart."

It is needless to say it was not long before she was found of the Good Shepherd and began to rejoice in God her Savior.

And now, in conclusion, I must add a word as to the importance and blessedness of thus leading souls into full salvation. When we lead a soul to Christ, we lead but one. When, however, like Joshua of old, we are able to lead a saint into the land that flows with milk and honey, we are the means of saving a thousand. The soul thus empowered becomes another Joshua, a center of light and blessing and power, and himself a winner of souls.

CHAPTER 12
# Idolatry

You shall have no other gods before Me. (Ex. 20:3)

The present volume, dealing as it does with the saving of men in heathen lands, would be incomplete without devoting a chapter to idolatry and its evils and making some reference as to how to deal with it.

It seems, however, impertinent to attempt within the limits of a dozen pages to deal with a subject so vast and varied as the great system of false worship in heathen lands. Experience in one country can, of course, give one no authority to speak *ex cathedra*; and yet a few general remarks may be of some help to young missionaries as they start out in their respective fields of service.

In a country like Japan, where idolatry is "swept and garnished," if not considerably embellished, and where other vices are so flagrant, it would almost appear as though heathenism were only an incident in the situation. Indeed, it is easy so to regard it, and yet not even here is that the case. Though it may be too much to say that idol worship is the *fons et origo* of all the evils we see about us, it is at any rate one of the stoutest fortresses of Satan, in which he has held captive for millennia myriads of the human race.

Idolatry has a variety of forms. So, too, has the cult of dealing with the dead, such as worship of saints, spiritualism, ancestor worship, etc. Whatever and howsoever many they be, they all rob God of His glory and His due. He has created the sons of men, that to Him, and Him alone, they may offer worship and thanksgiving, praise and prayer, honor and glory forever and ever.

Does all this appear mere platitude? Fifty years ago it might. But today, alas! so-called breadth of thought and charity of view challenges much of what I have written and puts an apostrophe and question mark after almost every statement. Natural religion (the generic term for heathen faiths) is at any rate by armchair professors regarded as a grand steppingstone to divine revelation! All talk of satanic agency is regarded as a mere fairy tale.

> And so they've voted the devil out,
> And of course the devil has gone;
> But simple people would like to know
> Who carries his business on!

The task before the soul-winner in heathen lands is threefold, as he sets himself to extricate the inquirer from the toils and snares of idol worship. These we may consider in order.

## 1. To Convict of Its Sinfulness

[When these people] say to you, "Why has the Lord pronounced all this great disaster against us? Or what is our iniquity? Or what is our sin that we have committed against the Lord our God?" then you shall say to them, "Because your fathers have forsaken Me," says the Lord, "they have walked after other gods and have served them, and worshipped them, and have forsaken Me and not kept My law." (Jer. 16:10-11)

In dealing with men and women in heathen lands, we need to use the greatest tact and grace. At times and under certain circumstances, sarcasm may be employed, though with extreme care; at others, a kindly smile at the folly of it all may help. But, generally speaking, while explaining the sinfulness of idol worship, we need to remember that they have never known, have never heard, have never had a chance, that they are taken captive by the devil at his will, that our forefathers were no better, and we, who are we that we should laugh and scold either at their folly or their sin? Paul at the Areopagus is a model for every missionary in every land. We may well weep rather than laugh, sorrow rather than chide, if we would turn them from dumb idols to serve the living God.

The Word of God provides us with ample instruction as to how to approach our task. One cannot read the prophet Isaiah without being impressed that the folly, no less than the wickedness, of "praying to a god that cannot save" (Isa. 45:20) is much emphasized. Again and again the prophet indulges in holy sarcasm, but then he is addressing an apostate people, and we are not. In any case, we need to use the Word of God if we would bring real conviction to the heart.

In speaking of idol worship, the Scriptures lay emphasis on three obvious facts.

1. The lifelessness of the heathen's god. "Dumb idols," says the Apostle (1 Cor. 12:2). A god who never speaks and who never answers, how shall it be a god to us? The inability to see or hear or speak is contrasted with the power of the Living God. "The God who answers by fire, He is God," said Elijah of old, as he faced the devotees of Baal.
2. The *powerlessness* of the heathen's god. Says Isaiah, "They have no knowledge, who carry the wood of their carved image, and pray to a god that cannot save . . . There is no other God besides Me, a just God and a Savior" (Isa. 45:20–21). Here is a further point of emphasis: the power to save. If a god cannot save from sin and fear of death, how can he be a god in whom to trust? This is the supreme test of all. Heathenism, of course, knows naught of any such thing. Sin is the one thing that idolatry is

indifferent to, at least in most of its forms. Yes, the God who saves, He is God.

3. The *sinfulness* of bowing down to a heathen god. Here is the most important fact of all. Idolatry is not only vanity; it is sin. The forsaking of the fount of living waters and hewing out for ourselves cisterns that can hold no water; the substitution of the creature for the Creator, in Whose hand our breath is, and Whom we have not glorified, this banishing of God from His own world, and making gods after our own covetous hearts, is of all things the most heinous of sins in His sight.

These are the simple means I would suggest in approaching a devotee of idols. Beware of metaphysics. Avoid argument. Insist on being practical. Press the battle to the gate. Make salvation from sin the ultimate test. Come back to that again and again. Let that be the issue, as it *always* is in the pages of Scripture. The Asiatic loves to be a philosopher in these matters. Insist that he be a shopkeeper if need be, or anything else of the kind that is plain and practical. Philosophers very rarely find God. Children and "mere sinners" are the successful ones in the race for heaven and in the search for eternal treasure.

## 2. To Insist on the Destruction of Idols and Dissociation from All Its Worship

You shall burn the carved images of their gods with fire; you shall not covet the silver or gold that is on them, nor take it for yourselves, lest you be snared by it; for it is an abomination to the Lord your God. Nor shall you bring an abomination into your house, lest you be doomed to destruction like it; but you shall utterly detest it and utterly abhor it, for it is an accursed thing. (Deut. 7:25-26)

As I have pointed out, there is a strange, unaccountable unwillingness on the part of the convert to destroy his idols and sever all connection with false worship, even after he has become a Christian. This, I know, is partly accounted for by fear of men. He hesitates to make himself peculiar and unlike his neighbor, and thus subject himself to petty persecution and ridicule.

But this does not altogether account for the facts. I can only account for it by the statement of the Holy Ghost that "the things which the Gentiles sacrifice they sacrifice to demons and not to God" (1 Cor. 10:20), and that behind the system of idolatry is a strange satanic power binding and holding its devotees.

The statements in the Old Testament are tremendous. The quotation I make from the Book of Deuteronomy is only one of a number, though this particular one was brought home to me with peculiar emphasis in the earlier days of my missionary life. A goodly number of idols and god-shelves, tobacco pipes, drinking cups, etc., had been given to me by converts as mementos of their repentance. Among them was a large image of Buddha, some 400 years old, which had been handed down to its owner as a family heirloom. These I had kept to show to friends as evidences of the power of God. On looking at them, a

CMS missionary from China who was visiting our home quietly observed, "Have you ever noticed particularly Deuteronomy 7:25–26?" I owned I had not, but on turning up the reference I made haste to commit the abominations to the cheerful flames in my garden.

When Christian converts themselves no longer worship at the temples or at their own god-shelf and have given up all faith therein, I have found in some cases an unwillingness to turn the "accursed thing" out of their homes on the plea that there is a grandfather or grandmother or uncle or aged parent to be considered. In some cases, such a plea may be valid, but in very many cases not. This lingering connection with idolatry does not necessarily mean that the man or woman in question is not a really converted person, as St. Paul's letter the Corinthian church shows, but it does indicate a low state of grace. It behooves a true shepherd of the flock to see to it that these snares and pitfalls are utterly destroyed.

Some time ago, the concubine of a wealthy man was brightly converted to God in our Mission Hall. She severed all her sinful connections and disposed of her idols and suffered much persecution from her sister, a very bigoted idolatress, who, however, not long afterwards, being taken seriously ill, turned to the true and living God on her deathbed, when she discovered that all her life long she had "prayed to a god that could not save." She was baptized, but her friends insisted on a Buddhist funeral.

She left behind her a magnificent shrine, worth perhaps £50 or £60, in the charge of her Christian sister. The

Buddhist priest made periodical visits for his usual perquisites. Mrs. H., the converted concubine, made no offerings thereat either of rice or flowers, but allowed her little boy to do so. One better instructed than she reproved her for allowing him and pointed out her sin before God. Almost at that moment, the pastor happened to call, to whom she unburdened her heart and suggested selling the "whole outfit" and giving the proceeds to the church.

Only two or three days before, another convert had done this very thing, though of course in the light of Deut. 7:25–26, we refused the money, telling him to give it to some work of charity. On the following day, still another married couple, knowing better, had chopped up their gods for firewood, a most sensible and practical transaction. With these instances in his mind, the pastor instructed Mrs. H. to bring her abomination to the Hall, which she did the following evening. After the prayer meeting, we made a bonfire and committed the shrine to its flames, warming body, soul, and spirit as we watched it disappear in smoke and ashes!

From the very beginning of a missionary's career, it is important that he should feel deeply, understand clearly, and speak plainly on this most important subject and insist on the destruction of these abominable things.

### 3. To Get Them Delivered

This kind does not go out except by prayer and fasting. (Matt. 17:21)

Are we convinced that heathen worship is satanic in its origin and maintained existence? Then obviously only one course is open to us: the way of praying in the Holy Ghost, if we would seek to get the captive freed from his captor. Human dialectic avails not here.

In the Epistle to the Ephesians, we read of divine power which operates in the heart of the believer.

1. As the power that lifts us *up* and seats us in heavenly places in Christ freed from sin and care and doubt and fear, the mighty power of *faith* (Eph. 1)
2. As the power that brings Christ *down* into our hearts, filling them with love to one another, yea, and to all—His mighty power of *love* (Eph. 3:16)
3. As the power that lifts us *up* again, when thus equipped with faith and love which is in Christ Jesus, to fight against principalities and powers— "the power of His might" it is called—the power of *prayer* in the Holy Ghost (Eph. 6:10, 18)

Here are the weapons of our warfare: faith in an ascended Lord to satisfy ourselves; love to His people and to the souls of the lost; and the power to pray and thus pluck them out of the hand of the mighty one, breaking the spell with which he bewitches the minds of his devotees. It is a battle, a real battle, not indeed with flesh and blood, but a spiritual conflict, taxing strength and nerve and heart to the uttermost.

I know of a country town in this land with a church accustomed to hearing the deepest spiritual truths. The pastor is a spiritual man. For several years, leaders of our

Convention work have gone to take special meetings, which last year I was deputed to conduct. Again there seemed a keen appreciation of all that I was able to declare, but all the time I was conscious that we were getting nowhere. Nothing definite was accomplished. The words of Ezekiel came continually to my mind. "Indeed, you are to them as a very lovely song of one who has a pleasant voice and can play well on an instrument; for they hear your words, but they do not do them" (Ezek. 33:32).

I began to make inquiries and found that in almost every Christian home the god-shelf remained (though they did not worship thereat), and that on the occasion of heathen festivals the Christians invariably gave their subscriptions to the priests. Hearing the state of affairs, I spoke with exceeding plainness and solemnity. Alas! I made no impression. They seemed to have no sense of conviction on the point whatever.

This year, three of our Japanese brethren, men full of the Holy Ghost, were invited to conduct the usual autumn meetings. For three days, taking an unoccupied cottage in the hills, they gave themselves to fasting and prayer. They continued night and day, getting very little sleep. On the fourth day, the meetings began, and God came down in great power. The first result was a glorious iconoclasm. The wretched idols were pulled down and committed to the flames, and house after house disposed of their abominations.

They afterwards declared, "Mr. Wilkes came here last year and spoke strongly to us about the matter, but for the

# IDOLATRY

life of us we could not imagine why he seemed so desperately in earnest on a matter which appeared to us at that time of little moment." I had used the Scriptures freely, and in great plainness of speech sought to show their sin—but what is a preacher if the Holy Ghost sent down from heaven is not with him? "This kind does not go out except by prayer and fasting," as our Japanese believed and proved. When He came in answer to their days of fasting and prayer, how swiftly did He convict and constrain to a true repentance!

Yes, idolatry is one of the great fortresses of the devil, and to extricate souls therefrom is not the play of a child.

CHAPTER 13
# Conclusion

. . . full of the Holy Spirit and wisdom . . . a man full of faith . . . Stephen, full of grace and power. (Acts 6:3, 5, 8)

Today is the day of substitutes. At no time more emphatically than now has there been such a fatal tendency to substitute quantity for quality; men for "a man"; organization for the Holy Spirit; education for the grace of God; money for spiritual power; and so-called salvation by character for redemption through Christ.

The Pope in bygone days, showing him all the glory and splendor of the Vatican, turned with pride to Thomas Aquinas and said, "We cannot say as Peter of old, 'Silver and gold I do not have.'"

"Nor yet," replied Thomas, "can we say, 'But what I do have I give you: In the name of Jesus Christ of Nazareth, rise up and walk' [Acts 3:6]."

In the foregoing pages, we have considered some of the requisites necessary for success in leading men and women to Christ: method and message, care in diagnosis, knowledge of men and things, acquaintance with the human heart through the Word and through inquiry of the soul, definiteness in dealing, concentration in presentation and appeal, assured conviction that a speedy harvest is possible, and a knowledge of the minimum of truth required for an appeal to the heart and conscience. Witnesses have been called to corroborate, scriptural proofs have been cited; and I trust that these things have suggested to our minds many other important considerations and kindred themes for inquiry and study.

And yet we have scarcely touched the heart of the subject at all. The one supreme and all-absorbing essential for success in this sacred, terrible, and yet blessed work, is the Holy Ghost. Without Him we have naught. He alone can convict of sin. He alone can reveal Christ and His atoning sacrifice. He alone is the mighty, convincing, converting power of God.

No knowledge of method or message will avail anything unless the message and messenger are full of the Holy Ghost. Here is the soul-winner's great secret; and ere we close this little volume I would devote a few pages to this, the most important part of the whole subject. The arm behind the sword, the brain behind the pen, the

CONCLUSION 183

heart behind the hand, the love behind the message—these are the forces that wound and win and speak and save. For the production of these spiritual forces, the Holy Spirit of the Living God alone avails.

I have a friend, an earnest Christian businessman living in one of these Eastern cities. Through the visit of an American evangelist, he was greatly stirred to see the need of personal soul winning. He sought first of all to prepare his own heart and life. He discovered much that had to be cleared out and put away. Letters of humiliating confession had to be dispatched. He set himself to his task with the utmost determination, and then when, as he thought, he had done all, he gathered a group of Christian friends about him and began to work.

He studied the question of personal evangelism in private and study circles. He searched his Bible, read all the books he could find, and at the same time went out to seek "that which was lost" (Matt. 18:11). He and his friends studied and labored thus the whole of one winter. At its close they met, and there, in confusion of face and intense disappointment, they had to confess to themselves and one another that they had caught nothing. That, apparently, was literally true. Not a single soul had been won to Christ. The secret had eluded him. Where could it be found? Why the failure, when he had paid the price, and that no little one, for the purchase of the treasure?

Almost despairing, he sought "to the law and to the testimony" (Isa. 8:20) again and determined to discover wherein lay the secret of power. For weeks he studied the theme of the Holy Ghost, for he had by this time become convinced that power belongs to God, and that this power is His Holy Spirit. Here again he nearly missed his way. From his conversion, there had been instilled into his mind the unscriptural notion that there was no such thing as an "endue[ment] with power from on high" subsequent to the new birth, and that with the exodus from Egypt came an immediate entrance into the promised land—if indeed there was any promised land at all this side of heaven.

As, however, with prayer and patient study, he sought God's way of power, he was brought to Galatians 3:13–14. Like a revelation, he saw the way of faith, and with a humbled, longing heart he dared to believe. The day and the hour are chronicled vividly in his mind when the Comforter came to abide. He was like a bird set free. Christ was revealed within. His heart was made clean. The temple of the Living God now welcomed and enthroned its rightful Sovereign and God. He was filled with the Holy Ghost. At once the Living Water began to flow from under the Throne of God and the Lamb. He became a winner of souls from that day forth.

When Stephen and the other deacons were called to their office, the condition of their appointment was that they should be filled with the Holy Ghost. This pregnant expression is set forth for us in four equally pregnant phrases: "full of . . . wisdom," "full of faith," "full of grace," and "full of . . . power" (Acts 6:3, 5, 8). Here are the four great secrets of the soul-winner, and them we may consider in their order.

## Full of Wisdom (Acts 6:3)

When Solomon came to this throne, that is what he sought, "A wise and understanding heart" (1 Kings 3:12).

First of all, it is a wisdom of *certitude.* The Holy Ghost seals to our consciousness the gracious things we read of and believe. We speak whereof we know. Christ is not only preached as the wisdom of God, but also experienced as such.

Secondly, it is the wisdom of *discernment.* We are equipped to know the hearts of men as never before. "I never met a man," says the biographer of William Bramwell, "who had such a deep and accurate knowledge of human nature and the operation of the Spirit of God." And if there was a man filled with the Holy Spirit, and an almost unparalleled winner of souls, during the last century, it was William Bramwell. It is a wisdom that "is justified by her children" (Matt. 11:19) that knows when to pipe and dance and when to mourn. This was the wisdom that made Solomon call for the sword that he might discern the whereabouts of love.

Thirdly, it is the wisdom of *inspiration* that knows how to use the Word of God. As with Stephen, our language will be the language of God's Book. I have heard both in prayer, preaching, and personal dealing the words of Scripture gushing from the heart like an artesian well, instinctively rising to the lips. The divinely inspired words appear peculiarly appropriate and powerful when uttered by one filled with the Holy Ghost. I have been astonished to see how swiftly the Holy Spirit, after coming to His temple, makes the Word of God dwell in the heart richly in all wisdom (Col. 3:16). To see the native worker thus enriched and made mighty to convict and convert is one of our greatest joys. The heart and mind and lips seem almost suddenly stored with the words of God. Herein is the wisdom of the winner of souls!

Similarly, in company with souls in prayer, I have again and again observed that those most filled with the Spirit intuitively make use of God's own words in addressing Him. Prayer and praise are most effective in harmony and power when expressed in the language that God the Holy Ghost has given us.

Finally, it is the wisdom of *witness* and testimony. "A true witness delivers souls" (Prov. 14:25). An ounce of testimony does more to convict and convert than a ton of sermons or theory.

On every hand the disciples went forth to be His witnesses. That is what men and women want to see and hear. The man filled with the Holy Ghost will be always ready to testify of what the Lord Jesus has done for him and is to him, like the Samaritan woman of old. The twelve theological students went into Sychar that day and brought nothing but a box of sandwiches for their Master. The woman saved brought a town full of people to His feet.

## Full of Faith (Acts 6:5)

Of all the evidence that proves a saint to be filled with the Spirit of God, this is most certain. Every true Christian has faith, but "fullness of faith" comes only with the fullness of the Holy Ghost. The strain and struggle to believe God has passed away, and in its place a constant sense of rest and assurance remains, gentle as the dew, slender as a thread at times may appear, but it abides sweet, persuasive, and assured. A conscious abiding in Christ may best describe it—a sense of safety, combined with a holy fear and trembling lest we should ever lose so sacred a trust or step outside the city of refuge, to be seized once more by the law, that great avenger of blood. Such is the inward state, the fountain from which the prayer of faith flows forth.

But fullness of faith, of course, means much more than all this. It means the power to believe for others as well as for oneself. Many know faith as the secret of their own spiritual life but have never seen it yet as the means for securing results in their ministry. Without it the Lord cannot work on our behalf. He waits till we actively, consciously, aggressively believe.

I remember when on furlough in England taking a series of meetings in a north-country parish. The vicar's wife was greatly blessed of God. The Lord Jesus was graciously revealed to her spiritual consciousness. She was filled with love and joy and peace and expected immediately that in her classes and in her parish work she would see the power of God convicting and converting sinners. She saw, however, very little of any such thing. Some six months later she wrote to me in trouble and disappointment about the matter, inquiring of the reason. I wrote back somewhat as follows: "The Lord never said, 'He who loves Me . . . out of his heart will flow rivers of living water,' but 'He who *believes* in Me . . . " (John 7:38).

Not long since, a devoted missionary, equally distressed at lack of fruit in his service, came to me inquiring why, though having the full assurance of faith for himself and having entered into the Land of Rest, enjoying the constant presence of the Lord, he saw but little results in his ministry. I sought to show him also that faith had to be exercised for this very thing. The faith that saves and the faith that sanctifies will not produce an automatic fruitfulness in service. Besides faith in God as Savior and Sanctifier, we have to exercise faith in Him as the mighty Worker. Faith in the blood of Christ—the price paid for the redemption of other souls—has to be exercised for others. The soul-winner who has never seen the need of faith thus will hardly be able to get others to believe and will in consequence have to lament a constant failure.

### Full of Grace (Acts 6:8)

When the Lord Jesus, full of the Holy Ghost, stood up to speak in the synagogue, it is said the people marveled at the gracious words that proceeded from His lips. He was full of grace. Fullness of grace is evident by graciousness

CONCLUSION

of *address*. Some of us have to contend with a naturally ungracious disposition and manner, but the grace of God can change even us. John Wesley was accustomed to observe that he never knew an instance of the grace of God being received and cherished in a man's heart where its transforming power did not soon manifest itself in a change of manners.

Fullness of grace will further manifest itself in our *message*. Grace always says *now;* grace always has hope for the vilest; grace realizes that salvation is of God and makes much of His promises and immediate willingness to save. The Lord Jesus is very large in the eyes of one who is full of grace; he loves to think and speak of a Savior that is always on hand to give and bless. Grace says continually that it is easy for God to bless us. Grace cries, "Today you will be with Me in Paradise," "Today salvation has come to this house," "Today this Scripture is fulfilled in your hearing," "Come, for all things are *now* ready" (Luke 23:43, 19:9, 4:21, 14:17). Yes! it is easy to know if a preacher of the Gospel is "full of grace."

But it is about another aspect of the fullness of grace that I want to speak more particularly—*purity of heart*. Much has been said and written in modern times about power for service. Many have sought it, and sought it in vain, because their eyes have been upon the coveted prize—*power*. God in His mercy has in many cases withheld so dangerous a gift. The soul that is not fully saturated with grace, becoming top-heavy with his load of power, will very soon totter to his fall and eternal undoing.

Who does not know the insidious danger of being used to influence and bless other men? As with Simon of old, the desire, not for the purifying presence of the Holy Ghost in the soul but merely for the power to communicate it to others, is a peril that lies nearer to the saint and soul-winner than he has any idea of (Acts 8).

The man who is filled with the Holy Ghost will not be constantly talking and thinking about baptisms of power. Nay, rather, filled with grace that humbles him into the dust, he will be ever conscious that he is and has nothing, He will desire that the Lord be glorified rather than he be used. His cry will be, "Lord, make me usable," rather than, "Use me."

A sense of the grace and goodness of God in Christ will be so paramount, that priceless as the privilege is of helping others, *this* can never again become the place whereon we offer the sacrifice of our time and talents unto God. Many of us, alas! have worshipped in that "high place"; many have bowed down to that secret idol, only to find that all power as well as grace has vanished as a dream in the night. That is the Delilah on whose lap many have slumbered, only to awake and find that the Philistines are upon them. They rise and discover that they are as weak as other men.

## Full of Power (Acts 6:8)

Knowledge is power; purity is power; faith is power. But here we read of a dynamic used in a specific sense, something other and more than the power of wisdom, purity, and faith.

# CONCLUSION

Now most people associate this in their minds with facility and incisiveness of speech to convict and convert sinners, as spoken from the pulpit or platform. This there may, and in most cases will be, though we need to remember that the convicting power on the day of Pentecost was poured through no eloquent lips of magnificent discourse. It rather flowed along the new-cut watercourses of simple testimony.

A study of the Word of God, moreover, discovers to us other forms of power than this—the power to endure (Col. 1:11), the power needed ere we can entertain and enthrone an indwelling Christ (Eph. 3:16). It is abundantly plain that the saint who intends to walk and work with God needs to be strengthened with might in the inner man.

Poetical, philosophical, social, and political Christs may dwell in heated heads and dreamy brains, but when the real, living Christ who dwells only in humble hearts comes to abide, that through us He may seek to win the souls He had redeemed, we shall need to be full of power by the Holy Ghost.

But the passage before us seems to speak of some other and more distinctive power than this, namely, the power to work miracles in the name of Jesus. Some have it in a marked and striking manner, where others equally saintly in life and walk have it not. I know of Japanese workers—very few, I admit—who have the gift of healing and are able to pray the prayer of faith over the sick.

I think an unbiased reading of the Acts of the Apostles will convince us that the power received on the day of

Pentecost was mainly the power to move the hand of God by prayer. It is of this latter I wish to speak—the power to pray, to *continue* in prayer and to *prevail.* I know of no more sure and certain evidence of being filled with the Holy Ghost than the possession of this power.

Not long since, a schoolmaster called to see me, longing to be filled with the Spirit of God. For two hours we searched the Word and talked; finally bowing in earnest prayer for the promised gift, he received and went his way rejoicing. Meeting him some time later, I inquired as to what God had done for him. As to that he was in no uncertainty.

He replied, "In the first place, I have the assurance of faith that I am wholly the Lord's such as I never before possessed." He was full of faith. "In the next place," he added, "the Word of God has become my meat and drink. I cannot but devour it." He was full of wisdom. "And thirdly," he continued, "I have such joy in prayer and such liberty and power to continue in intercession for others that I scarce know myself." He was full of power.

Says William Bramwell, "One thing is needful, which is continual prayer. All will fail unless you labor in this way. Let the times be as frequent as possible and the manner as fervent as possible. Full of expectation, look for the promise and believe for the blessing. Be mighty in this duty; you will be strongly tempted to neglect prayer. Satan can continue his authority with all persons who do not give themselves to prayer."

No one will be a soul-winner who is not full of power to pray.

# CONCLUSION

It is this power to pray, to continue in it and to prevail, that is at the bottom of every form of spiritual power at our disposal. More particularly does it lie at the root of success in winning souls to Christ.

This is the sign that we are filled with the Holy Ghost. "The soul-winner must pray in secret; he must get alone with God and pour his heart into his Heavenly Father's ear, with intercessions and pleadings and arguments, if he would have good success. There is no substitute for much wide-awake, expectant, secret waiting on God for the outpouring of the Holy Spirit; the gift of wisdom, strength, courage, hope, faith, discernment of times and spirits, and a glowing, burning, comprehensive message from Him to the people.

"Here, then, is the secret of success, closet communion, and counselings and conversations with God Who is our Father and Who can and will no more turn away from us when we come in the spirit of an obedient and affectionate child, than can the sunlight when we throw open the windows and doors and stand in its beam."

Only the man of prayer will be full of power. Only the man full of the Holy Ghost will be a man of prayer.

Here I bring this little volume to a close and earnestly entreat any young missionary who may happen to read its pages to seek above and beside and beyond all equipment in instruction, method, or address that power which alone belongs to God. The need of the mission field is not more men, more money, or more education, or more brains; still less is it more organization or more method.

It is spiritual leadership, and "spiritual leadership," as a modern soul-winner used of God has observed, is "not won nor established by promotion, but by many prayers, and tears, and confessions of sin, and heart searchings and humblings before God, and self-surrender, and a courageous sacrifice of every idol, and a bold and deathless and uncompromising, uncomplaining embracing of the Cross, and an eternal, unfaltering looking unto Jesus crucified . . . . Spiritual leaders are not made by man, nor any combination of men. Neither conferences nor synods nor councils can make them, but only God."

If we are daily and continually filled with the Holy Ghost, we never need fear that we shall grow old or become "back numbers," for, as the same writer goes on to say, "I know men—old men—*full of God* who were persecuted in their prime for Jesus' sake, but who had salt in themselves, and kept sweet, and delighted themselves in the Lord, whose bow abides in strength, whose sun is shining in fullness of splendor, and who are filling the world with divine messages that men are eager to hear. Know this, that long service and experience will not save you from becoming 'back numbers' but God in you will. God is always up to date. It is God that men need."

The supreme demand of this perishing world is men full of wisdom, full of faith, full of grace, and full of power. It is such men that God is seeking, and to such men, humbled at His presence, He will appear and give them their commissions to serve in the dark places of the earth. That commission straight from the lips of our ascended Lord, and that alone, will prove a dynamic to the soul.

We end as we began, with the Word of the Living God:

> But rise and stand on your feet; for I have appeared to you for this purpose, to make you a *minister* and a *witness* both of the things which you have seen and of the things which I will yet reveal to you. I will deliver you from the Jewish people, as well as from the Gentiles, to whom I now send you, to open their eyes and to turn them from darkness to light, and from the power of Satan to God, that they may receive forgiveness of sins and an inheritance among those who are sanctified by faith in Me. (Acts 26:16–18)

That such a commission should ever be given to sinners saved by the grace of God, such as we, we can only bow in the deepest abasement and say Hallelujah and again Hallelujah!

www.ingramcontent.com/pod-product-compliance
Lightning Source LLC
Chambersburg PA
CBHW071342080526
44587CB00017B/2932